AMAZED BY
GRACE

AMAZED BY GRACE

EDITED BY ELIZABETH KEA

W PUBLISHING GROUP™

www.wpublishinggroup.com

A Division of Thomas Nelson, Inc.
www.ThomasNelson.com

Published by W Publishing Group, a Division of Thomas Nelson, Inc., P.O. Box 141000, Nashville, Tennessee 37214.

Unless otherwise noted, all Scripture is from THE NEW KING JAMES VERSION. Copyright © 1979, 1980, 1982, Thomas Nelson, Inc., Publishers.

Scripture quotations marked NIV are taken from the HOLY BIBLE: NEW INTERNATIONAL VERSION®. Copyright © 1973, 1978, 1984 by International Bible Society. Used by permission of Zondervan Publishing House. All rights reserved.

Scripture quotations marked KJV are taken from THE KING JAMES VERSION of the Bible.

"Grace," from AMAZING GRACE by Kathleen Norris, copyright © 1998 by Kathleen Norris. Used by permission of Riverhead Books, an imprint of Penguin Group (USA) Inc.

"Will God Forgive What I'm About to Do?" "Five Polluted Words," and "Dispatch from the Culture Wars": from FINDING GOD IN UNEXPECTED PLACES by Philip Yancey, copyright © 1995 by Philip Yancey. Used by permission of Ballantine Books, a division of Random House, Inc.

Library of Congress Cataloging-in-Publication Data

Amazed by grace / edited by Elizabeth Kea.
    p. cm.
 ISBN 0-8499-1807-3
 1. Grace (Theology) I. Kea, Elizabeth Bonner, 1976– II. Title.
BT761.3.A45 2003
234—dc22   2003017821

Printed in the United States of America
04 05 06 07 BVG 5 4 3

Contents

HOW SWEET THE SOUND

Grace Greater Than Our Sin / Julia H. Johnston   3

Grace, Enough for Me / Edwin O. Excell   4

Grace, 'Tis a Charming Sound /
    Philip Doddridge and Augustus M. Toplady   5

Grace Is Always a Surprise / Stormie Omartian   7

Victors / Donald McCullough   8

Growing in Grace / Hannah Whitall Smith   9

Amazing Grace / John Newton   11

The Prodigal Son (Luke 15:11–32)   13

Amazed by Grace / James Montgomery Boice   15

His Grace Is Sufficient for Me / Leila N. Morris   17

Call It Grace / Max Lucado   18

Grace / Kathleen Norris   19

Saved by Grace / Karl Barth   21

Humble Beginnings / Brian D. McLaren   23

From Sin Set Free / Amy Carmichael   24

Grace Communicated / Jonathan Edwards   25

The Motivation of God's Salvation / Charles Stanley   26

Righteous Grace / Horatius Bonar 27

It Is Well with My Soul / Horatio Spafford 31

Too Good to Be True / Madeleine L'Engle 33

Ungracious Grace / G. K. Chesterton 34

The Day That I Was Crowned / Emily Dickinson 35

JESUS: THE PERSON OF GRACE

He Became Flesh / Max Lucado 39

He Is Grace Indeed / John Bunyan 40

Must Be a Woe / Emily Dickinson 41

Grace Is Jesus / Barbara Johnson 42

Look to Christ / Robert Murray M'Cheyne 44

How Sweet the Name / John Newton 45

And God Became Man /
    Saint Alphonsus Maria de Liguori 47

Alas and Did My Savior Bleed / Isaac Watts 49

The Woman Caught in Adultery (John 8:2–11) 51

A Violent Grace / Michael Card 52

Clothed in His Righteousness / John Calvin 54

A Sinful Woman Forgiven (Luke 7:36–50) 55

His Mercy and Love / Charles Dickens 57

Quick-Eyed Love / George Herbert 58

I Came for the Sick (Matthew 9:9–13) 59

Christ Our Mediator / John Owen   60

Christ and the Pagan / John Bannister Tabb   64

BY GRACE ALONE

Dependent on Grace / Susanna Wesley   69

Nothing but the Blood / Robert Lowry   70

Striving Less / Cynthia Heald   72

Free Grace / J. I. Packer   74

Give Up and Wake Up / Nicole Johnson   77

The Hospital / Charles Spurgeon   79

Alive in Christ (Ephesians 2:4–10, 19–22)   81

A View of Grace / Daniel Defoe   82

Rock of Ages / Augustus M. Toplady   83

Relying on God's Grace / R. C. Sproul   85

Generous Grace / Bryan Chapell   86

The Seal of Grace / Michael Green   89

The Fountain of Grace / Dwight L. Moody   91

The Mover / A Puritan Prayer   93

Clothed with Christ / Max Lucado   95

By Grace Through Faith / Charles Spurgeon   97

Out of the Depths / Martin Luther   100

SUFFICIENT GRACE

Grace Enough / George MacDonald   105

Come to the Throne of Grace / Cynthia Heald   106

Grace Active / A Puritan Prayer   108

Timely and Needed Help / F. B. Meyer   110

My Shepherd Will Supply My Need / Isaac Watts   115

In Boldness I Come / John Chrysostom   117

From Every Stormy Wind / Hugh Stowell   118

Grace upon Grace / Max Lucado   120

There's a Wideness in God's Mercy /
    Frederick William Faber   121

Restraining Grace / Samuel Rutherford   123

A Hymn to God the Father / John Donne   125

Grace for Living / Dwight L. Moody   126

Do Thou for Me / Amy Carmichael   131

The Death of Sin (Romans 6:8–11, 14; 11:6)   133

Approach, My Soul, the Mercy Seat / John Newton   134

But for the Grace of God / Martin Luther   136

He Giveth More Grace / Annie Johnson Flint   138

GRACE THAT TRANSFORMS

The Grace Which Costs / Dietrich Bonhoeffer   141

Will God Forgive What I'm About to Do? / Philip Yancey   144

Grace Reigning / Scotty Smith　　148

Come, Thou Fount of Every Blessing / Robert Robinson　　149

The Most Amazing Grace / Os Guinness　　151

Leave Your Life of Sin / James Montgomery Boice　　154

The Grace of Wonder / Brennan Manning　　157

Manifold Grace / Amy Carmichael　　161

All of Grace / Os Guinness　　162

Appreciating God's Grace / Thomas à Kempis　　165

Effective Grace (Ephesians 3:1–12)　　167

The Covenant of Grace / Andrew Murray　　168

Blessed Assurance / Martin Luther　　173

Grace for Service / Dwight L. Moody　　174

Galilean Grace / Max Lucado　　176

A Drop of Grace / John Tauler　　178

A Holy Sonnet / John Donne　　180

Further Up and Further In / C. S. Lewis　　181

The Reign of Grace / Scotty Smith　　183

INSTRUMENTS OF GRACE

Beggars in Need of Bread / Max Lucado　　187

Five Polluted Words / Philip Yancey　　188

A Prayer for Grace / Jane Austen　　193

The Law of Love / Cynthia Heald   194

The Temper / George Herbert   196

Love Your Enemies (Matthew 5:38–48)   198

Responding to Grace / Brennan Manning   199

How the Great Guest Came / Edwin Markham   202

The Divine Nature of Grace / Thomas à Kempis   205

Dispatch from the Culture Wars / Philip Yancey   208

Abounding Grace for Abounding Work / Andrew Murray   211

Grace to Others / Jerry Bridges   214

Grace at Work / Charles Spurgeon   216

The Potter and the Clay / George Whitefield   220

Make Me an Instrument / Francis of Assisi   223

Notes   225
Acknowledgments   227

How Sweet the Sound

The sun of righteousness will rise
with healing in its wings.
And you will go out and leap
like calves released from the stall.

—Malachi 4:2 (NIV)

Grace is not about finishing last or first;
it is about not counting.

—Philip Yancey

Grace Greater Than Our Sin

JULIA H. JOHNSTON

Marvelous grace of our loving Lord,
Grace that exceeds our sin and our guilt!
Yonder on Calvary's mount outpoured,
There where the blood of the Lamb was spilled.

Sin and despair, like the sea waves cold,
Threaten the soul with infinite loss;
Grace that is greater, yes, grace untold,
Points to the refuge, the mighty cross.

Dark is the stain that we cannot hide.
What can we do to wash it away?
Look! There is flowing a crimson tide,
Brighter than snow you may be today.

Marvelous, infinite, matchless grace,
Freely bestowed on all who believe!
You that are longing to see His face,
Will you this moment His grace receive?

Grace, Enough for Me

EDWIN O. EXCELL

In looking through my tears one day,
I saw Mount Calvary;
Beneath the cross there flowed a stream
Of grace, enough for me.

Grace is flowing from Calvary,
Grace as fathomless as the sea,
Grace for time and eternity,
Grace, enough for me.

While standing there, my trembling heart,
Once full of agony,
Could scarce believe the sight I saw
Of grace, enough for me.

When I beheld my every sin
Nailed to the cruel tree,
I felt a flood go through my soul
Of grace, enough for me.

When I am safe within the veil,
My portion there will be,
To sing through all the years to come
Of grace, enough for me.

Grace, 'Tis a Charming Sound

PHILIP DODDRIDGE AND AUGUSTUS M. TOPLADY

Grace, 'tis a charming sound,
Harmonious to mine ear;
Heaven with the echo shall resound,
And all the earth shall hear.

Grace first contrived the way
To save rebellious man;
And all the steps that grace display
Which drew the wondrous plan.

Grace first inscribed my name
In God's eternal book;
'Twas grace that gave me to the Lamb,
Who all my sorrows took.

Grace led my roving feet
To tread the heavenly road;
And new supplies each hour I meet,
While pressing on to God.

Grace taught my soul to pray
And made mine eyes o'erflow;
'Twas grace which kept me to this day,
And will not let me go.

Grace all the work shall crown,
Through everlasting days;
It lays in heaven the topmost stone,
And well deserves the praise.

O let Thy grace inspire
My soul with strength divine
May all my powers to Thee aspire,
And all my days be Thine.

Grace Is Always a Surprise

STORMIE OMARTIAN

I've spent fifteen years learning to understand what was accomplished on the cross, and it simply means that Jesus took all that I have coming to me—pain, failure, confusion, hatred, rejection, and death—and gave me all that He had coming to Him—all His wholeness, healing, love, acceptance, peace, joy, and life. Because of God's grace, all we have to do is say, "Jesus, come live in me and be Lord over my life."

Grace and mercy are much alike. Grace happens when God refrains from punishing a person who is guilty. Mercy is God's compassion for our misery beyond what may be expected. We need both.

If it weren't for God's grace *and* mercy, we wouldn't even be saved for the Bible tells us, "by *grace* you have been saved" (Eph. 2:8) and "according to His mercy He saved us" (Titus 3:5). Before we met Jesus we were "guilty" and "miserable," but His "grace" and "mercy" have saved us.

Grace has to do with it all being *Him. He* does it. Not us. Grace is always a surprise. You think it's not going to happen, and it does. Pastor Jack Hayford teaches about grace that "When the humble say, 'I don't have it and I can't get it on my own,' God says, 'I've got it and I'm going to give it to you.' That's God's grace."

—from *Finding Peace for Your Heart*

Victors

DONALD MCCULLOUGH

Grace means that in the middle of our struggle the referee blows the whistle and announces the end of the game. We are declared winners and sent to the showers. It's over for all huffing, puffing piety to earn God's favor; it's finished for all sweat-soaked straining to secure self-worth; it's the end of all competitive scrambling to get ahead of others in the game. Grace means that God is on our side and thus we are victors regardless of how well we have played the game. We might as well head for the showers and the champagne celebration.

—from *Waking from the American Dream*[1]

Growing in Grace

HANNAH WHITALL SMITH

What is meant by growing in grace? It is difficult to answer this question because so few people have any conception of what the grace of God really is. To say that it is free, unmerited favor, only expresses a little of its meaning. It is the wondrous, boundless love of God, poured out upon us without stint or measure, not according to our deserving, but according to His infinite heart of love, which passeth knowledge, so unfathomable are its heights and depths.

I sometimes think we give a totally different meaning to the word "love" when it is associated with God, from that we so well understand in its human application. But if ever human love was tender and self-sacrificing and devoted; if ever it could bear and forbear; if ever it could suffer gladly for its loved ones; if ever it was willing to pour itself out in a lavish abandonment for the comfort or pleasure of its objects—then infinitely more is Divine love tender and self-sacrificing and devoted, and glad to bear and forbear, and to suffer, and to lavish its best of gifts and blessings upon the objects of its love. Put together all the tenderest of love you know of, dear reader, the deepest you have ever felt, and the strongest that has ever been poured out upon you, and heap upon it all the love of all the loving human hearts in the world, and then multiply it by infinity, and you will begin perhaps to have some faint glimpses of what the love of God in Christ Jesus is. And this is grace. And to be planted in grace is to live in the very heart of this love, to be enveloped by it, to be steeped in it, to revel in it, to know nothing else but love only and love always, to grow day by day in the knowledge of it, and in faith in it, to intrust everything to its care, and to have no shadow of a doubt but that it will surely order all things well.

To grow in grace is opposed to all self-dependence, to all self-effort, to all legality of every kind. It is to put our growing, as well as everything else, into the hands of the Lord, and leave it with Him. It is to be so satisfied with our Husbandman, and with His skill and wisdom, that not a question will cross our minds as to His modes of treatment or His plan of cultivation. It is to grow as the lilies grow, or as the babes grow, without a care and without anxiety; to grow by the power of an inward life principle that cannot help but grow; to grow because we live and therefore must grow; to grow because He who has planted us has planted a growing thing, and has made us to grow.

—from *The Christian's Secret of a Happy Life*

Amazing Grace

JOHN NEWTON

Amazing grace! How sweet the sound
That saved a wretch like me!
I once was lost, but now am found;
Was blind, but now I see.

'Twas grace that taught my heart to fear,
And grace my fears relieved;
How precious did that grace appear
The hour I first believed.

Through many dangers, toils and snares,
I have already come;
'Tis grace hath brought me safe thus far,
And grace will lead me home.

The Lord has promised good to me,
His Word my hope secures;
He will my Shield and Portion be,
As long as life endures.

Yea, when this flesh and heart shall fail,
And mortal life shall cease,
I shall possess, within the veil,
A life of joy and peace.

The earth shall soon dissolve like snow,
The sun forbear to shine;
But God, Who called me here below,
Shall be forever mine.

When we've been there ten thousand years,
Bright shining as the sun,
We've no less days to sing God's praise
Than when we'd first begun.

The Prodigal Son

LUKE 15:11–32

Then [Jesus] said: "A certain man had two sons. And the younger of them said to his father, 'Father, give me the portion of goods that falls to me.' So he divided to them his livelihood. And not many days after, the younger son gathered all together, journeyed to a far country, and there wasted his possessions with prodigal living.

"But when he had spent all, there arose a severe famine in that land, and he began to be in want. Then he went and joined himself to a citizen of that country, and he sent him into his fields to feed swine. And he would gladly have filled his stomach with the pods that the swine ate, and no one gave him anything.

"But when he came to himself, he said, 'How many of my father's hired servants have bread enough and to spare, and I perish with hunger! I will arise and go to my father, and will say to him, "Father, I have sinned against heaven and before you, and I am no longer worthy to be called your son. Make me like one of your hired servants."'

"And he arose and came to his father. But when he was still a great way off, his father saw him and had compassion, and ran and fell on his neck and kissed him. And the son said to him, 'Father, I have sinned against heaven and in your sight, and am no longer worthy to be called your son.' But the father said to his servants, 'Bring out the best robe and put it on him, and put a ring on his hand and sandals on his feet. And bring the fatted calf here and kill it, and let us eat and be merry; for this my son was dead and is alive again; he was lost and is found.' And they began to be merry.

"Now his older son was in the field. And as he came and drew near to the house, he heard music and dancing. So he called one of the servants and asked what these things meant. And he said to him, 'Your brother has come, and because he has received him safe and sound, your father has killed the fatted calf.'

"But he was angry and would not go in. Therefore his father came out and pleaded with him. So he answered and said to his father, 'Lo, these many years I have been serving you; I never transgressed your commandment at any time; and yet you never gave me a young goat, that I might make merry with my friends. But as soon as this son of yours came, who has devoured your livelihood with harlots, you killed the fatted calf for him.' And he said to him, 'Son, you are always with me, and all that I have is yours. It was right that we should make merry and be glad, for your brother was dead and is alive again, and was lost and is found.'"

Amazed by Grace

JAMES MONTGOMERY BOICE

It has always been like this.

Do you remember Thomas? He was the doubting disciple, the one who said that he would not believe in Jesus' resurrection unless he should see the wounds in Christ's hands and be able to thrust his hand into the wound in Christ's side. Why should Thomas have been saved? After all, his cynical words expressed utter disbelief, not faith. Yet even Thomas was surprised by grace when Jesus, instead of condemning him or abandoning him, appeared to him and invited him to perform his empirical test. Instead of doing it, instead of putting his finger or hand in Christ's wounds, Thomas was overwhelmed by grace and fell at Jesus' feet, exclaiming, "My Lord and my God!" (John 20:28 NIV).

And how about Peter? Peter had boasted of being able to stand by Jesus even unto death. How little he knew himself! That very night he denied the Lord three times. But although he was rightly ashamed of what he had done and wept bitterly afterwards, Jesus did not cast him off. Instead Jesus came to Peter to recommission him to service.

"Simon son of John, do you love me?" Jesus asked.

"Yes," said Peter.

"Take care of my sheep," said Jesus. Jesus repeated the question and charge three times, corresponding to Peter's three denials (John 21:15–17). Amazing! It was not only grace in salvation that was shown to Peter. It was grace commissioning him to useful service.

And Paul, the first great persecutor of the church? He took his hatred of Christians to the point of securing the condemnation and death of Stephen, the first martyr. And when he had accomplished this, he left for Damascus with the thought of arresting and likewise punishing the believers there. If ever anyone deserved a swift retaliatory judgment, it was Paul. Yet Paul, too, was surprised by grace, as Jesus stopped him on his fiercely bigoted path, calling, "Saul, Saul, why do you persecute me?" (Acts 9:4 NIV). And when Paul responded in faith, recognizing that the one he was persecuting was Christ, the very Son of God, Jesus commissioned him to be the first great missionary to the Gentiles. "I will rescue you from your own people and from the Gentiles. I am sending you to them to open their eyes and turn them from darkness to light, and from the power of Satan to God, so that they may receive forgiveness of sins and a place among those who are sanctified by faith in me" (Acts 26:17–18 NIV).

Surprised by grace? Yes! That is exactly it. "Surprised by grace" is the story of all who have found salvation through faith in Jesus Christ.

—from *The Glory of God's Grace*

His Grace Is Sufficient for Me

LEILA N. MORRIS

"I've anchored my soul in the Haven of Rest";
I've pillowed my head on the dear Savior's breast;
I'm trusting His promise of mercy so free;
Fear not, "For My grace is sufficient for thee."

At home or abroad, on the land or the sea,
God's wonderful grace is sufficient for me;
I'm finding it true that where'er I may be,
His grace is sufficient for me,
For me, for me, His grace is sufficient for me.

Wherever my lot upon earth may be cast,
Mid storm and mid tempest He holdeth me fast;
No harm can betide while His dear face I see,
And cling to the hand that was wounded for me.

The billows in fury around me may beat;
The "Cleft in the Rock" is my blessèd retreat;
My Shield and Defender forever is He;
The Savior Whose grace is sufficient for me.

And when I have finished life's voyage at last,
When safe in the harbor my anchor is cast,
The theme of my praises forever shall be,
God's grace, which is always sufficient for me.

Call It Grace

MAX LUCADO

You may be decent. You may pay taxes and kiss your kids and sleep with a clear conscience. But apart from Christ you aren't holy. So how can you go to heaven?

Only believe. Accept the work already done, the work of Jesus on the cross.

Accept the goodness of Jesus Christ. Abandon your own works and accept his. Stand before God in his name, not yours.

It's that easy? There was nothing easy about it at all. The cross was heavy, the blood was real, and the price was extravagant. It would have bankrupted you or me, so he paid it for us. Call it simple. Call it a gift. But don't call it easy.

Call it what it is. Call it grace.

—from *A Gentle Thunder*

Grace

Jacob's theophany, his dream of angels on a stairway to heaven, strikes me as an appealing tale of unmerited grace. Here's a man who has just deceived his father and cheated his brother out of his inheritance. But God's response to finding Jacob vulnerable, sleeping all alone in the open country, is not to strike him down for his sins but to give him a blessing.

Jacob wakes from the dream in awe, exclaiming, "Surely the Lord is in this place—and I did not know it!" For once, his better instincts take hold, and he responds by worshipping God. He takes the stone that he'd kept close by all night, perhaps to use as a weapon if a wild animal, or his furious brother Esau, were to attack him, and sets it up as a shrine, leaving it for future travelers, so that they, too, will know that this is a holy place, the dwelling place of God.

Jacob's exclamation is one that remains with me, a reminder that God can choose to dwell everywhere and anywhere we go. One morning this past spring I noticed a young couple with an infant at an airport departure gate. The baby was staring intently at other people, and as soon as he recognized a human face, no matter whose it was, no matter if it was young or old, pretty or ugly, bored or happy or worried-looking he would respond with absolute delight.

It was beautiful to see. Our drab departure gate had become the gate of heaven. As I watched that baby play with any adult who would allow it, I felt as awe-struck as Jacob, because I realized that this is how God looks at us, staring into our faces in order to be

HOW SWEET THE SOUND • 19

delighted, to see the creature he made and called good, along with the rest of creation. And, as Psalm 139 puts it, darkness is as nothing to God, who can look right through whatever evil we've done in our lives to the creature made in the divine image.

I suspect that only God, and well-loved infants, can see this way. But it gives me hope to think that when God gazed on the sleeping Jacob, he looked right through the tough little schemer and saw something good, if only a capacity for awe, for recognizing God and worshipping. That Jacob will worship badly, trying to bargain with God, doesn't seem to matter. God promises to be with him always.

Peter denied Jesus, and Saul persecuted the early Christians, but God could see the apostles they would become. God does not punish Jacob as he lies sleeping because he can see in him Israel, the foundation of a people. God loves to look at us, and loves it when we will look back at him. Even when we try to run away from our troubles, as Jacob did, God will find us, and bless us, even when we feel most alone, unsure if we'll survive the night. God will find a way to let us know that he is with us *in this place,* wherever we are, however far we think we've run. And maybe that's one reason we worship—to respond to grace. We praise God not to celebrate our own faith but to give thanks for the faith God has in us. To let ourselves look at God, and let God look back at us. And to laugh, and sing, and be delighted because God has called us his own.

—from *Amazing Grace: A Vocabulary of Faith*

Saved by Grace

Someone once said to me, "I need not go to church. I need not read the Bible. I know already what the church teaches and what the Bible says: 'Do what is right and fear no one!'" Let me say this at this point: if this were the message at stake, I would most certainly not have come here. My time is too precious and so is yours. To say that, neither prophets nor apostles, neither Bible, Jesus Christ nor God are needed. Anybody is at liberty to say this to himself. By the same token this saying is void of any new, of any very special and exciting message. It does not help anyone. I have never seen a smile on the face of a person reassuring himself with this kind of talk. . . . Let us hear therefore what the Bible says and what we as Christians are called to hear together: By grace you have been saved! No man can say this to himself. Neither can he say it to someone else. This can only be said by God to each one of us. It takes Jesus Christ to make this saying true. . . .

You probably all know the legend of the rider who crossed the frozen Lake of Constance by night without knowing it. When he reached the opposite shore and was told whence he came, he broke down, horrified. This is the human situation when the sky opens and the earth is bright, when we may hear: By grace you have been saved! In such a moment we are like that terrified rider. When we hear this word we involuntarily look back, do we not, asking ourselves: Where have I been? Over an abyss, in mortal danger! What did I do? The most foolish thing I ever attempted! What happened? I was doomed and miraculously escaped and now I am safe! . . .

Look once again to Jesus Christ in His death upon the cross. Look and try to understand that what He did and suffered, He did and suffered for you, for me, for us all. He carried our sin, our captivity and our suffering, and did not carry it in vain. *He carried it away.* He acted as the captain of us all. He broke through the ranks of our enemies. He has already won the battle, our battle. All we have to do is to follow Him, to be victorious with Him. Through Him, in Him we are saved. Our sin no longer has any power over us. Our prison door is open. . . . When He, the Son of God, sets us free, we are *truly* free.

—from *Deliverance to the Captives*

Humble Beginnings

Brian D. McLaren

That kind of reflection—where we see ourselves and think again about what direction we want to take in the future, sure that it is a very different direction than we've taken so far—often puts us in a frame of heart and mind where we experience God. Why is this? Here's my guess: At those moments where we freely admit our wrongs, we are as close as we ever get to being truly humble. At those moments there is a response that comes from God, a personal response so natural and strong that it can't be stopped, like a hand instantly reaching out to a companion who falls, or like a mother's instinctive turn when she hears her child's cry. The words the theologians use for this pure, spontaneous response is "grace" —amazing grace.

Grace is what a father feels (and a son receives) when he catches his son doing something wrong, and the boy (instead of defending himself or blaming his little brother or making an excuse or telling a pathetic lie to cover it up) bursts into tears and says, "I'm sorry." Punishment seems unnecessary; a stern word even seems out of place. The father takes the boy in his arms and simply says, "It's okay. I love you."

When we experience the grace of God in this way, it can be one of life's most significant events.

—from *Finding Faith*

From Sin Set Free

Amy Carmichael

The shadows of the underworld
Compassed about my guilty soul;
And thunderbolts were on me hurled,
And lightnings flashed. And on a scroll
Was written down, without, within,
The secret of my hidden sin.

Without, within, I saw it stand,
In clearest words accusing me,
Till, as it were, a wounded hand
Annulled its record, set me free.
With that the stormy wind did cease.
A voice commanded: there was peace.

O Savior stricken for my sin,
O God who gavest Him to grief,
O Spirit who didst woo and win
My troubled soul to seek relief,
O Love revealed at Calvary,
Thy glory lights eternity!

—from *Made in the Pans*

Grace Communicated

Jonathan Edwards

If we make no difficulty of allowing that God did immediately make the whole universe at first, and caused it to exist out of nothing, and that every individual thing owes its being to an immediate, voluntary, arbitrary act of Almighty power, why should we make a difficulty of supposing that He has still something immediately to do with the things that He has made, and that there is an arbitrary influence still that God has in the creation that He has made?

And if it be reasonable to suppose it with respect to any part of the Creation, it is especially so with respect to reasonable creatures, who are the highest part of the Creation, next to God, and who are most immediately made for God, and have Him for their next Head, and are created for the business wherein they are mostly concerned. And above all, in that wherein the highest excellency of this highest rank of beings consist, and that wherein he is most conformed to God, is nearest to Him, and has God for his most immediate object. . . .

That principle of grace that is in the hearts of the saints is as much a proper communication or participation of the Spirit of God, the Third Person in the Trinity, as that breath that entered into these bodies is represented to be a participation of the wind that blew upon them.

—from *Treatise on Grace*

The Motivation of God's Salvation

CHARLES STANLEY

We did nothing to motivate God to save us. His motivation was intrinsic. It came from within His nature. He saw our plight and felt compassion for us. Anyone who has stopped along the road to pick up a stray dog or move a fallen bird's nest to a safe place has in a limited way mirrored the compassion expressed by God in salvation.

Paul explains this even further with his parenthetical remark, "By grace you have been saved." The Greek form of the term *grace* implies that grace is the "instrument" used to accomplish salvation.[2] In other words, if one were to ask God, "God, how did You save me?" He would answer, "Grace."

Grace summarizes the entire salvation process. It encapsulates the sending of Christ, the offer of forgiveness, His crucifixion, His resurrection, and His ascension. Why grace? Because grace indicates unmerited favor; it suggests an undeserved expression of kindness and goodwill. The whole of salvation is just that—an undeserved gift. From start to finish, salvation is by grace. We have now answered two basic questions.

QI: Why did God save us?

AI: He loved us.

Q2: How did God save us?

A2: By grace; by an undeserved series of events enacted for our benefit.

—from *Eternal Security*

Righteous Grace

HORATIUS BONAR

Let us keep in mind that this grace is the grace of a righteous God; it is the grace of one who is Judge as well as Father. Unless we see this we shall mistake the gospel, and fail in appreciating both the pardon we are seeking, and the great sacrifice through which it comes to us. No vague forgiveness, arising out of mere paternal love, will do. We need to know what kind of pardon it is; and whether it proceeds from the full recognition of our absolute guiltiness by him who is to "judge the world in righteousness." The right kind of pardon comes not from love alone, but from law; not from good nature, but from righteousness; not from indifference to sin, but from holiness.

The inquirer who is only half in earnest overlooks this. His feelings are moved, but his conscience is not roused. Hence he is content with very vague ideas of God's mere compassion for the sinner's unhappiness. To him human guilt seems but human misfortune, and God's acquittal of the sinner little more than the overlooking of his sin. He does not trouble himself with asking how the forgiveness comes, or what is the real nature of the love which he professes to have received. He is easily soothed to sleep, because he has never been fully awake. He is, at the best, a stony-ground hearer; soon losing the poor measure of joy that he may have got; becoming a formalist; or perhaps a trifler with sin; or it may be, a religious sentimentalist.

But he whose conscience has been pierced is not so easily

satisfied. He sees that the God, whose favor he is seeking, is holy as well as loving; and that he has to do with righteousness as well as grace. Hence the first inquiry that he makes is as to the righteousness of the pardon which the grace of God holds out. He must be satisfied on this point, and see that the grace is righteous grace, ere he can enjoy it all. The more alive he is to his own unrighteousness, the more does he feel the need of ascertaining the righteousness of the grace which we make known to him. . . .

Here the work of Christ comes in; and the cross of the Sin-bearer answers the question which conscience has raised—"Is it righteous grace?" It is this great work of propitiation that exhibits God as "the just God, yet the Saviour"; not only righteous in spite of His justifying the ungodly, but righteous in doing so. It shows salvation as an act of righteousness; nay, one of the highest acts of righteousness that a righteous God can do. It shows pardon not only as the deed of a righteous God, but as the thing which shows how righteous He is, and how He hates and condemns the very sin that He is pardoning. . . .

Had it not been for this dying, grace and guilt could not have looked each other in the face; God and the sinner could not have come nigh; righteousness would have forbidden reconciliation; and righteousness, we know, is as divine and real a thing as love. Without this exception, it would not have been right for God to receive the sinner nor safe for the sinner to come.

But now, mercy and truth have met together; now grace is righteousness, and righteousness is grace. This satisfies the sinner's conscience, by showing him righteous love for the unrighteous and unlovable. It tells him, too, that the reconciliation brought about in this way shall never be disturbed, either in this life or that which is to come. It is righteous reconciliation, and will stand every test, as well as last throughout eternity. The peace of conscience thus secured will be trial-proof, sickness-proof, deathbed-proof, judgment-proof. Realizing this, the chief of sinners can say, "Who is he that condemneth?"

What peace for the stricken conscience is there in the truth that Christ died for the ungodly; and that it is of the ungodly that the righteous God is the Justifier! The righteous grace thus coming to us through the sin-bearing work of the "Word made flesh," tells the soul, at once and forever, that there can be no condemnation for any sinner upon earth, who will only consent to be indebted to this free love of God, which, like a fountain of living water, is bursting freely forth from the foot of the Cross.

Just, yet the Justifier of the ungodly! What glad tidings are here! Here is grace; God's free love to the sinner; divine bounty and goodwill, altogether irrespective of human worth or merit. For this is the scriptural meaning of that often misunderstood word "grace."

This righteous free love has its origin in the bosom of the Father, where the only begotten has His dwelling. It is not produced by anything out of God himself. It was man's evil, not his good, that called it forth. It was not the drawing to the like, but to the unlike; it was light attracted by darkness, and life by death. It does not wait for our seeking, it comes unasked as well as undeserved. It is not our faith that creates it or calls it up; our faith realizes it as already existing in its divine and manifold fullness. Whether we believe it or not, this righteous grace exists, and exists for us. Unbelief refuses it; but faith takes it, rejoices in it, and lives upon it. Yes, faith takes this righteous grace of God, and, with it, a righteous pardon, a righteous salvation, and a righteous heirship of the everlasting glory.

—from *God's Way of Peace*

It Is Well with My Soul

HORATIO SPAFFORD

When peace, like a river, attendeth my way,
When sorrows like sea billows roll;
Whatever my lot, Thou has taught me to say,
It is well, it is well, with my soul.

It is well, with my soul,
It is well, with my soul,
It is well, it is well, with my soul.

Though Satan should buffet, though trials should come,
Let this blest assurance control,
That Christ has regarded my helpless estate,
And hath shed His own blood for my soul.

My sin, oh, the bliss of this glorious thought!
My sin, not in part but the whole,
Is nailed to the cross, and I bear it no more,
Praise the Lord, praise the Lord, O my soul!

For me, be it Christ, be it Christ hence to live:
If Jordan above me shall roll,
No pang shall be mine, for in death as in life
Thou wilt whisper Thy peace to my soul.

But, Lord, 'tis for Thee, for Thy coming we wait,
The sky, not the grave, is our goal;
Oh trump of the angel! Oh voice of the Lord!
Blessed hope, blessed rest of my soul!

And Lord, haste the day when my faith shall be sight,
The clouds be rolled back as a scroll;
The trump shall resound, and the Lord shall descend,
Even so, it is well with my soul.

Too Good to Be True

MADELEINE L'ENGLE

Isaiah knew himself to be mortal and flawed, but he had the child's courage to say to the Lord, "Here I am. Send me." And he understood the freedom which the Spirit can give us from ordinary restrictions when he wrote, "When you pass through deep waters, I am with you; when you pass through rivers, they will not sweep you away; walk through fire and you will not be scorched, through flames and they will not burn you." He may not have had this understanding before he wrote those words, for such understanding is a gift when we let go, and listen. I think I looked up this passage because I dreamed that a friend reached into the fireplace and drew out a living coal and held it in his hand, looking at its radiance, and I wondered at him because he was not burned.

It may be that we have lost our ability to hold a blazing coal, to move unfettered through time, to walk on water, because we have been taught that such things have to be earned; we should deserve them; we must be qualified. We are suspicious of grace. We are afraid of the very lavishness of the gift.

But a child rejoices in presents!

—from *Walking on Water*

Ungracious Grace

G. K. CHESTERTON

All other philosophies say the things that plainly seem to be true; only [Christianity] has again and again said the thing that does not seem to be true, but is true. Alone of all creeds it is convincing where it is not attractive; it turns out to be right. . . . Theosophists for instance will preach an obviously attractive idea like reincarnation; but if we wait for its logical results, they are spiritual superciliousness and the cruelty of caste. For if a man is a beggar by his own prenatal sins, people will tend to despise the beggar. But Christianity preaches an obviously unattractive idea, such as original sin; but when we wait for its results, they are pathos and brotherhood, and a thunder of laughter and pity; for only with original sin we can at once pity the beggar and distrust the king. Men of science offer us health, an obvious benefit; it is only afterwards that we discover that by health, they mean bodily slavery and spiritual tedium. Orthodoxy makes us jump by the sudden brink of hell; it is only afterwards that we realize that jumping was an athletic exercise highly beneficial to our health. It is only afterwards that we realize that this danger is the root of all drama and romance. The strongest argument for the divine grace is simply its ungraciousness.

—from *Orthodoxy*

The Day That I Was Crowned

EMILY DICKINSON

The Day that I was crowned
Was like the other Days—
Until the Coronation came—
And then—'twas Otherwise—

As Carbon in the Coal
And Carbon in the Gem
Are One—and yet the former
Were dull for Diadem—

I rose, and all was plain—
But when the Day declined
Myself and It, in Majesty
Were equally—adorned—

The Grace that I—was chose—
To Me—surpassed the Crown
That was the Witness for the Grace—
'Twas even that 'twas Mine—

Jesus:
The Person
of Grace

And the Word became flesh and dwelt among us,
and we beheld His glory, . . .
full of grace and truth.

—JOHN 1:14

If the veil be fully rent, and the blood be of
divine value and potency, and the mercy-seat be
really the place of grace, and the High Priest
full of love to the sinner, then every shadow of a
reason for doubt is swept utterly away.

—HORATIUS BONAR

He Became Flesh

MAX LUCADO

We want to know how long God's love will endure. . . . Not just on Easter Sunday when our shoes are shined and our hair is fixed. . . . Not when I'm peppy and positive and ready to tackle world hunger. Not then. Even I like me then.

I want to know how he feels about me when I snap at anything that moves, when my thoughts are gutter-level, when my tongue is sharp enough to slice a rock. How does he feel about me then? . . .

Can anything separate us from the love Christ has for us?

God answered our question before we asked it. So we'd see his answer, he lit the sky with a star. So we'd hear it, he filled the night with a choir; and so we'd believe it, he did what no man had ever dreamed. He became flesh and dwelt among us.

He placed his hand on the shoulder of humanity and said, "You're something special."

—from *In the Grip of Grace*

He Is Grace Indeed

JOHN BUNYAN

Thou Son of the Blessed, what grace was manifest in Thy condescension! Grace brought Thee down from heaven; grace stropped Thee of Thy glory; grace made Thee poor and despicable; grace made Thee bear such burdens of sin, such burdens of sorrow, such burdens of God's curse as are unspeakable.

O Son of God, grace was in all Thy tears; grace came bubbling out of Thy side with Thy blood; grace came forth with every word of Thy sweet mouth; grace came out where the whip smote Thee, where the thorns pricked Thee, where the nails and spear pierced Thee. O blessed Son of God, here is grace indeed! unsearchable riches of grace! unthought of riches of grace! grace to make angels wonder, grace to make sinners happy, grace to astonish devils!

—from *The Riches of Bunyan*

Must Be a Woe

EMILY DICKINSON

Must be a woe—
A loss or so—
To bend the eye
Best Beauty's way—

But once aslant
It notes Delight
As difficult
As Stalactite

A Common Bliss
Were had for less—
The price—is
Even as the Grace—

Our lord—thought no
Extravagance
To pay—a Cross—

Grace Is Jesus

Grace is one of those "theological" words that we say we believe in and even count on, but sometimes it's good to consider what grace really *does* mean in a world where the gloomees are always out to get you. As Lewis Smedes says, God's grace can make life all RIGHT despite the fact that everything is obviously all WRONG. . . . Grace is the reality of God entering history—and our lives—to make things right at the very center.

Grace does not stand for an escape mechanism, some kind of all-expense-paid trip to Disneyland because God knows we can't afford to go ourselves. Grace has nothing to do with Disneylands, Fantasy Islands, magical cures, or instant solutions.

You may have seen the acrostic on grace that puts it all in perspective:

> God's
> Riches
> At
> Christ's
> Expense

Jesus never used the word *grace*. God left that for Paul, but if you want to describe grace in one word it is *Jesus*.

Grace (Jesus) is the answer for our guilt and failure.

Grace (Jesus) is the strength we need to cope with life.

Grace (Jesus) is the promise that gives us the hope that keeps us going.

—from *Pack Up Your Gloomees in a Great Big Box,*
Then Sit on the Lid and Laugh!

Look to Christ

Robert Murray M'Cheyne

Look to Christ; for the glorious Son of God so loved lost souls, that He took on Him a body and died for us—bore our curse, and obeyed the law in our place. Look to Him and live. You need no preparation, you need no endeavors, you need no duties, you need not strivings, you only need to look to Him and live.

How Sweet the Name

JOHN NEWTON

How sweet the name of Jesus sounds
In a believer's ear!
It soothes his sorrows, heals his wounds,
And drives away his fear.

It makes the wounded spirit whole,
And calms the troubled breast;
'Tis manna to the hungry soul,
And to the weary, rest.

Dear Name, the Rock on which I build
My Shield and Hiding Place,
My never-failing Treasury filled
With boundless stores of grace.

By Thee my prayers acceptance gain,
Although with sin defiled;
Satan accuses me in vain,
And I am owned a child.

Jesus, my Shepherd, Brother, Friend,
My Prophet, Priest, and King,
My Lord, my Life, my Way, my End,
Accept the praise I bring.

Weak is the effort of my heart,
And cold my warmest thought;
But when I see Thee as Thou art,
I'll praise Thee as I ought.

Till then I would Thy love proclaim
With every fleeting breath,
And may the music of Thy Name
Refresh my soul in death.

And God Became Man

SAINT ALPHONSUS MARIA DE LIGUORI

Because our first parent Adam had rebelled against God, he was driven out of paradise and brought on himself and all his descendants the punishment of eternal death. But the Son of God, seeing man thus lost and wishing to save him from death, offered to take upon Himself our human nature and to suffer death Himself, condemned as a criminal on a cross. "But my Son," we may imagine the eternal Father saying to Him, "think of what a life of humiliations and sufferings Thou wilt have to lead on earth. Thou wilt have to be born in a cold stable and laid in a manger, the feeding trough of beasts. While still an infant, Thou wilt have to flee into Egypt, to escape the hands of Herod. After Thy return from Egypt, Thou wilt have to live and work in a shop as a lowly servant, poor and despised. And finally, worn out with sufferings, Thou wilt have to give up Thy life on a cross, put to shame and abandoned by everyone." "Father," replies the Son, "all this matters not. I will gladly bear it all, if only I can save man."

What should we say if a prince, out of compassion for a dead worm, were to choose to become a worm himself and give his own life blood in order to restore the worm to life? But the eternal Word has done infinitely more than this for us. Though He is the sovereign Lord of the world, He chose to become like us, who are immeasurably more beneath Him than a worm is beneath a prince, and He was willing to die for us, in order to win back for us the life of divine grace that we had lost by sin. When He saw that all the other gifts which He had bestowed on us were not sufficient to induce us to repay His love with love, He became man Himself and gave Himself all to us. "The Word was made flesh and dwelt among us"; "He loved us and delivered Himself up for us."

Alas and Did My Savior Bleed

ISAAC WATTS

Alas! and did my Savior bleed
And did my Sovereign die?
Would He devote that sacred head
For such a worm as I?

Thy body slain, sweet Jesus, Thine—
And bathed in its own blood—
While the firm mark of wrath divine,
His Soul in anguish stood.

Was it for crimes that I had done
He groaned upon the tree?
Amazing pity! grace unknown!
And love beyond degree!

Well might the sun in darkness hide
And shut his glories in,
When Christ, the mighty Maker died,
For man the creature's sin.

Thus might I hide my blushing face
While His dear cross appears,
Dissolve my heart in thankfulness,
And melt my eyes to tears.

But drops of grief can ne'er repay
The debt of love I owe:
Here, Lord, I give my self away
'Tis all that I can do.

The Woman Caught in Adultery

JOHN 8:2–11

Early in the morning [Jesus] came again into the temple, and all the people came to Him; and He sat down and taught them. Then the scribes and Pharisees brought to Him a woman caught in adultery. And when they had set her in the midst, they said to Him, "Teacher, this woman was caught in adultery, in the very act. Now Moses, in the law, commanded us that such should be stoned. But what do You say?" This they said, testing Him, that they might have something of which to accuse Him.

But Jesus stooped down and wrote on the ground with His finger, as though He did not hear. So when they continued asking Him, He raised Himself up and said to them, "He who is without sin among you, let him throw a stone at her first." And again He stooped down and wrote on the ground.

Then those who heard it, being convicted by their conscience, went out one by one, beginning with the oldest even to the last. And Jesus was left alone, and the woman standing in the midst. When Jesus had raised Himself up and saw no one but the woman, He said to her, "Woman, where are those accusers of yours? Has no one condemned you?" She said, "No one, Lord." And Jesus said to her, "Neither do I condemn you; go and sin no more."

MICHAEL CARD

Imagine it with me.

Jesus is standing there stripped, shackled, and alone in the circle. The legionnaire steps forward, opens his reach, and begins. The scourges hiss through the air in a wide arc and sink with a thud in Christ's skin.

The crowd howls.

The scourges rise again and again in the soldier's fist. And fall. And rise again.

Soldiers sneer and spit. The scourges hiss and thud into purple flesh. Blood flows. God's chosen people scream for more.

The tormentor grunts and sweats, but keeps reaching back for that terrible, wide arc.

Jesus crumples. Guards rush to jerk Him to His feet. The scourges rise again, and fall.

Look! The righteous anger of God, diverted for all time, is pouring down on this man, His Son.

But the fault is mine, and I must look away.

It is one thing to speak in theological terms about an obligatory sacrifice for a fallen world. It is an entirely different thing to stand in the presence of brutal men and their instruments of torture and try to watch, realizing that Jesus endured all that and more for you and me.

Yet His pain was the prelude to the outpouring of God's favor. By enduring the violence in that circle of hate, Jesus accomplished a costly exchange. With each blow, He carried away our grief and our brokenness and bought back for us—for that howling mob and for every person since—the treasures of grace.

"By his wounds we are healed," wrote Isaiah. Healing through wounding; wholeness through brokenness. That is the way of the cross—the way of Jesus. It is the method of an upside-down kingdom, whose king dies for his subjects.

> *Surely he took up our infirmities*
> *and carried our sorrows,*
> *yet we considered him stricken by God,*
> *smitten by him, and afflicted.*
> *He was crushed for our iniquities;*
> *the punishment that brought us peace was upon him,*
> *and by his wounds we are healed.* (Isa. 53:4–5)

—from *A Violent Grace*

Clothed in His Righteousness

JOHN CALVIN

This is the wonderful exchange which, out of His measureless benevolence, He has made with us; that becoming Son of man with us, He has made us sons of God with Him; that, by taking on our mortality, He has conferred His immortality upon us; that, accepting our weakness, He has strengthened us by His power; that, receiving our poverty unto Himself, He has transferred His wealth to us; that, taking the weight of our iniquity upon Himself (which oppressed us), He has clothed us with His righteousness.

A Sinful Woman Forgiven

Then one of the Pharisees asked Him to eat with him. And He went to the Pharisee's house, and sat down to eat. And behold, a woman in the city who was a sinner, when she knew that Jesus sat at the table in the Pharisee's house, brought an alabaster flask of fragrant oil, and stood at His feet behind Him weeping; and she began to wash His feet with her tears, and wiped them with the hair of her head; and she kissed His feet and anointed them with the fragrant oil.

Now when the Pharisee who had invited Him saw this, he spoke to himself, saying, "This Man, if He were a prophet, would know who and what manner of woman this is who is touching Him, for she is a sinner." And Jesus answered and said to him, "Simon, I have something to say to you." So he said, "Teacher, say it."

"There was a certain creditor who had two debtors. One owed five hundred denarii, and the other fifty. And when they had nothing with which to repay, he freely forgave them both. Tell Me, therefore, which of them will love him more?" Simon answered and said, "I suppose the one whom he forgave more." And He said to him, "You have rightly judged."

Then He turned to the woman and said to Simon, "Do you see this woman? I entered your house; you gave Me no water for My feet, but she has washed My feet with her tears and wiped them with the hair of her head. You gave Me no kiss, but this woman has not ceased to kiss My feet since the time I came in. You did not anoint

JESUS: THE PERSON OF GRACE • 55

My head with oil, but this woman has anointed My feet with fragrant oil. Therefore I say to you, her sins, which are many, are forgiven, for she loved much. But to whom little is forgiven, the same loves little." Then He said to her, "Your sins are forgiven."

And those who sat at the table with Him began to say to themselves, "Who is this who even forgives sins?" Then He said to the woman, "Your faith has saved you. Go in peace."

His Mercy and Love

CHARLES DICKENS

One of the Pharisees begged Our Saviour to go into his house and eat with him. And while Our Saviour sat eating at the table, there crept into the room a woman of that city who had led a bad and sinful life, and was ashamed that the Son of God should see her; and yet she trusted so much to His goodness and His compassion for all who having done wrong were truly sorry for it in their hearts, that, by little and little, she went behind the seat on which He had sat, and dropped down at His feet, and wetted them with her sorrowful tears; then she kissed them, and dried them on her long hair, and rubbed them with some sweet-smelling ointment she had brought with her in a box. Her name was Mary Magdalene.

When the Pharisee saw that Jesus permitted this woman to touch Him, he said within himself that Jesus did not know how wicked she had been. But Jesus Christ, who knew his thoughts, said to him, "Simon"—for that was his name—"if a man had debtors, one of whom owed him only fifty pence, and he forgave them, both, their debts, which of those two debtors do you think would love him most?" Simon answered, "I suppose that one whom he forgave most." Jesus told him he was right, and said, "As God forgives this woman so much sin, she will love Him, I hope, the more." And He said to her, "God forgives you!" The company who were present wondered that Jesus Christ has power to forgive sins. But God had given it to Him. And the woman, thanking Him for all His mercy, went away.

Quick-Eyed Love

GEORGE HERBERT

Love bade me welcome: yet my soul drew back,
Guilty of dust and sin.
But quick-eyed Love, observing me grow slack
From my first entrance in,
Drew nearer to me, sweetly questioning
If I lacked anything.

"A guest," I answered, "worthy to be here":
Love said, "You shall be he."
"I, the unkind, ungrateful? Ah, my dear,
I cannot look on thee."
Love took my hand, and smiling did reply,
"Who made the eyes but I?"

"Truth, Lord; but I have marred them; let my shame
Go where it doth deserve."
"And know you not," says Love, "who bore the blame?"
"My dear, then I will serve."
"You must sit down," says Love, "and taste my meat."
So I did sit and eat.

I Came for the Sick

MATTHEW 9:9–13

As Jesus passed on from there, He saw a man named Matthew sitting at the tax office. And He said to him, "Follow Me." So he arose and followed Him.

Now it happened, as Jesus sat at the table in the house, that behold, many tax collectors and sinners came and sat down with Him and His disciples. And when the Pharisees saw it, they said to His disciples, "Why does your Teacher eat with tax collectors and sinners?" When Jesus heard that, He said to them, "Those who are well have no need of a physician, but those who are sick. But go and learn what this means: 'I desire mercy and not sacrifice.' For I did not come to call the righteous, but sinners, to repentance."

Christ Our Mediator

JOHN OWEN

His obedience was not for Himself but for us. We were obliged to obey and could not. He was not obliged to obey, but by a free act of His own will, did. God gave Him this honor; that He should obey for the whole church, so that "by one Man's obedience many will be made righteous" (Rom. 5:19). The reason why I say that God gave Him this honor and glory is because His obedience was to stand instead of our obedience in the matter of justification. His obedience, being absolutely perfect, revealed the holiness of God in the law. The Ten Commandments written on tablets of stone were glorious. But how much more glorious they became when written in the hearts of believers. But only in the holiness and obedience of Christ was this full glory seen. And this obedience is no small part of His glory. Through His human nature the glory of God's holiness was fully revealed by His perfect obedience.

Furthermore, Christ was perfectly obedient in the face of all difficulties and oppositions. Although He had no sin in him to hinder His obedience as we have, yet outwardly He was confronted with much that would turn Him from the path of obedience. Temptations, sufferings, reproaches, and contradictions were hurled at Him. So "though He was a Son, yet He learned obedience by the things which He suffered" (Heb. 5:8).

But the glory of His obedience becomes more wonderful when we realize who He was who thus obeyed God. He was none other than the Son of God made man. He who was in heaven, above all,

Lord of all, lived in the world, having no earthly glory or reputation, obliged to obey the whole law of God perfectly. He, to whom prayer was made, prayed Himself night and day. He, whom all the angels of heaven and all creatures worshipped, fulfilled all the duties which the worship of God required. He who was Lord and master of the house became the lowliest servant in the house, performing all menial duties. He that made all men, in whose hand they are all as clay is in the hand of the potter, observed among them the strictest rules of justice, in giving to everyone his due, and out of love giving good things to the undeserving. This is what makes the obedience of Christ so mysterious and glorious.

The glory of Christ is also to be seen in His sufferings. "Ought not the Christ to have suffered these things and to enter into His glory?" asked the risen Lord (Luke 24:26). But how can we begin to think of the sufferings of Christ?

We might see Him under the weight of God's wrath and the curse of the law, taking upon Himself and on His whole soul the utmost that God had ever threatened to sin or sinners. We might see Him in His agony and bloody sweat, in His strong cries and supplications, when He was sorrowful unto death and filled with horror at the sight of those things which were coming upon Him, the dreadful trial He was about to enter. We might see Him wrestling with all the powers of darkness, the rage and madness of men, and suffering all this in His soul, His body, His name, His reputation, His goods, and His life. Some of these sufferings were inflicted directly by God, others came from devils and wicked men, acting according to the determinate counsel of God. We might see Him praying, weeping, crying out, bleeding, dying, making His soul an offering for sin (Isa. 53:7–8).

Lord, what is man that you are so mindful of him? And the son of man that you visit him? Who has known your mind, or who has been your counselor? O the depths of the riches both of the wisdom and the knowledge of God! How unsearchable are His judgements, and His ways past finding out! What shall we say to these things? That God did not spare His Son, but gave Him up to death, and all the sufferings associated with that death, for such poor lost sinners! That for our sakes the eternal Son of God should submit Himself to all that our sinful natures were liable to, and our sins deserved, that we might be delivered!

How glorious the Lord Jesus Christ is in the eyes of believers! When Adam sinned, he stood ashamed, afraid, trembling, as one ready to perish forever under the severe displeasure of God. Death was what he deserved, and he fully expected the sentence to be immediately carried out. In this state, the Lord Jesus in the promise comes to him, and says, "Poor creature! How terrible is your condition! How deformed you are now! What has become of the beauty, the glory of that image of God in which you were created? See how you have taken upon yourself the monstrous shape and image of Satan? And yet your present sorrow, your physical return to dust and darkness, is in no way to be compared with what is to follow. Eternal distress lies before you. But now, look up and behold Me, and you will have a glimpse of what infinite wisdom, love, and grace have purposed for you. Do not continue to hide from Me. I will take your place. I will bear your guilt and suffer that punishment which would sink you eternally into the hideous depths of hell. I will pay for what I never took. I will be made a curse for you so that you may be eternally blessed." In the same vein the Lord Christ speaks to all convicted sinners when He invites them to come to Him.

This is how the Lord Christ is presented in the gospel as "clearly portrayed among you as crucified" (Gal. 3:1). This is how the glory of His sufferings shines forth.

—from *The Glory of Christ*

Christ and the Pagan

JOHN BANNISTER TABB

I had no God but these,
The sacerdotal Trees,
And they uplifted me.
"I hung upon a Tree."

The sun and moon I saw,
And reverential awe
Subdued me day and night.
"I am the perfect Light."

Within a lifeless Stone—
All other gods unknown—
I sought Divinity.
"The Corner-Stone am I."

For sacrificial feast,
I slaughtered man and beast,
Red recompense to gain.
"So I, a Lamb, was slain.

"Yea; such My hungering Grace
That wheresoe'er My face
Is hidden, none may grope
Beyond eternal Hope." [1]

BY
GRACE
ALONE

For by grace you have been saved through faith,
and that not of yourselves; it is the gift of God.
—EPHESIANS 2:8

The greater perfection a soul aspires after,
the more dependent it is upon divine grace.
—BROTHER LAWRENCE

While Jesus calls each of us to a more perfect life,
we cannot achieve it on our own. To be alive is to
be broken; to be broken is to stand in need of grace.
It is only through grace that any of us could dare to
hope that we could become more like Christ.
—BRENNAN MANNING

Dependent on Grace

SUSANNA WESLEY

You can no more do anything in your own strength than you can remove mountains or shape the solid foundations of the earth. 'Tis true God did at first bestow on reasonable beings sense, perception, and reason, but sin hath so weakened these powers that, unless divine grace restore them and renew the mind, they are in a manner perfectly useless, or at least will not serve to the end for which they were given.

Nothing but the Blood

ROBERT LOWRY

What can wash away my sin?
Nothing but the blood of Jesus;
What can make me whole again?
Nothing but the blood of Jesus.

Oh! precious is the flow
That makes me white as snow;
No other fount I know,
Nothing but the blood of Jesus.

For my pardon, this I see,
Nothing but the blood of Jesus;
For my cleansing this my plea,
Nothing but the blood of Jesus.

Nothing can for sin atone,
Nothing but the blood of Jesus;
Naught of good that I have done,
Nothing but the blood of Jesus.

This is all my hope and peace,
Nothing but the blood of Jesus;
This is all my righteousness,
Nothing but the blood of Jesus.

Now by this I'll overcome—
Nothing but the blood of Jesus,
Now by this I'll reach my home—
Nothing but the blood of Jesus.

Glory! Glory! This I sing—
Nothing but the blood of Jesus,
All my praise for this I bring—
Nothing but the blood of Jesus.

Striving Less

CYNTHIA HEALD

Trying to be perfect, wanting to please God, serving the body of Christ adequately—I often find that all these desires become blurred and I grow confused about how much or how little I must *do*. I don't always bridle my tongue; I rarely visit orphans and widows; I don't love impartially. I assume that I must try harder and do more to make up for my lack of obedience.

At this point Grace exclaims, "No! You now live in my realm of freedom, and you have the ever-present strength and help of the Holy Spirit. You must not try harder; you must strive less. You must acknowledge your helplessness and total dependence upon the Spirit for your guidance, your area of service, and your ability to love. You are created for good works, but they must flow out of your abiding communion with the living Vine."

Just as Mary of Bethany sat at the feet of Jesus listening to His words (while Martha was serving anxiously), Mary could not help but rise up and serve her Lord. It was her love for Jesus that moved her to abide in Him. As she abided, she was prompted to take her alabaster jar of perfume to anoint the Lord for burial— an incredible act of service that will always be told in remembrance of her.

True service always finds its source in loving our Savior, wanting to hear His Word, and then promptly obeying. As we listen to the Lord in faith with a willing heart, He can use us and produce His fruit in us. Our major work is to trust, abide, and obey. This is freedom from the law, and it is freedom to serve. My trust and faith in walking in the Spirit, and my love for the Lord, will assure my good works.

—from *Becoming a Woman of Grace*

Free Grace

J. I. PACKER

Those who study the printed sermons of worthy expositors of the old gospel, such as Bunyan, . . . or Whitefield or Spurgeon, will find that in fact they hold forth the Saviour and summon sinners to Him with a fullness, warmth, intensity and moving force unmatched in Protestant pulpit literature. And it will be found on analysis that the very thing which gave their preaching its unique power to overwhelm their audiences with broken-hearted joy at the riches of God's grace—and still gives it that power, let it be said, even with hard-boiled modern readers—was their insistence on the fact that grace is *free*. They knew that the dimensions of Divine love are not half understood till one realizes that God need not have chosen to save nor given his Son to die; nor need Christ have taken upon him vicarious damnation to redeem men, nor need He invite sinners indiscriminately to Himself as He does; but that all God's gracious dealings spring entirely from His own free purpose. . . .

To the question: what must I do to be saved? the old gospel replies: believe on the Lord Jesus Christ. To the further question: what does it mean to believe on the Lord Jesus Christ? its reply is: it means knowing oneself to be a sinner, and Christ to have died for sinners; abandoning all self-righteousness and self-confidence, and casting oneself wholly upon Him for pardon and peace; and exchanging one's natural enmity and rebellion against God for a spirit of grateful submission to the will of Christ through the renewing of one's heart by the Holy Ghost. And to the further question still: how am I to go about believing on Christ and repenting if I have no natural ability to do these things? it answers: look to Christ, speak to Christ, cry to Christ, just as you are; confess your sin, your impenitence, your unbelief, and cast yourself on His mercy; ask Him to give you a new heart, working in you true repentance and firm faith; ask Him to take away your evil heart of unbelief and to write His law within you, that you may never henceforth stray from Him. Turn to Him and trust Him as best you can, and pray for grace to turn and trust more thoroughly; use the means of grace expectantly, looking to Christ to draw near to you as you seek to draw near to Him; watch, pray, read and hear God's Word, worship and commune with God's people, and so continue till you know in yourself beyond doubt that you are indeed a changed being, a penitent believer, and the new heart which you desired had been put within you. The emphasis in this advice is on the need to call upon Christ directly, as the very first step.

> "Let not conscience make you linger,
> nor of fitness fondly dream;
> All the fitness He requireth
> Is to feel your need of Him"—

so do not postpone action till you think you are better, but honestly confess your badness and give yourself up here and now to the Christ who alone can make you better; and wait on Him till His light rises in your soul, as Scripture promises that it shall do.

Anything less than this direct dealing with Christ is disobedience of the gospel. Such is the exercise of spirit to which the old evangel summons its hearers. "I believe—help thou mine unbelief": this must become their cry.

—from the Introduction to
The Death of Death in the Death of Christ

Give Up and Wake Up

NICOLE JOHNSON

I have fallen asleep on God on more occasions than I can count. I have tried to memorize chapters of Scripture and found that I've killed so many brain cells trying to be thin and holy that I'm no longer able. I thought that Jesus said, "Come unto Me, all you who are weary and heavy laden, and I will give you more to *do* than anyone else!" But Jesus didn't say that. He promised me rest. But I couldn't find it. My constant struggle to be "godly" left me tired, empty, lonely on the inside, and ready to give up. . . .

I had worked for God and yet withheld my heart from Him. I'd sought to please Him, like a father who is hard to please, and missed that He was pleased with me. I tried to do so many things *for* God that I missed being *with* God. Where was the goodness in that? I was the keeper of the covenant. I was the one making the sacrifice. I thought what Jesus did for me paled in comparison to what I was doing for Him! God was so pleased to see me surrender, He probably laughed. I think He got tired just watching me. I discovered that the Christian life is not about trying harder. It is not about keeping it all together. It is about trusting in the One who can keep it all together. Martin Luther said that we show whether or not we believe the gospel by what we do when we sin. If we just roll up our sleeves and try harder, we are not walking with Jesus. If we all can do it ourselves, what do we need Him for?

When I gave up, I began to wake up. I felt the gentle stirring in my soul to respond to God. He whispered to me, "Jesus came to give you life." *Life? What is life if it isn't running all the time?* Peace—real peace on the inside, from all of this climbing, striving, and worrying. Joy—unabashed delight in life, regardless of the circumstances. Love—foundational, unconditional, never-ending love. I didn't have to work for these things, I just had to surrender to them. I had to stop long enough to let them overtake me. Again and again.

—from *Fresh-Brewed Life*

The Hospital

CHARLES SPURGEON

We know a place in England where bread is served to everyone who asks. All you have to do is knock on the door of St. Cross Hospital and bread is offered.

Jesus Christ so loves sinners that He has built His own St. Cross Hospital, where all hungry sinners have to do is knock. No, even better, Jesus has attached a bath to this Hospital of the Cross. Whenever souls are dirty and filthy, all they need to do is go there and be washed. The fountain is always full and effectual. Every sinner who ever came found that this bath washed away their stains. Sins that were scarlet and crimson disappeared and the sinner became whiter than snow.

As if this were not enough, a wardrobe is also attached to this Hospital of the Cross. Simply by asking, sinners may be clothed from head to foot. If they want to be soldiers, they are not given ordinary garments, but armor to cover them fully, and a sword and a shield.

Nothing good will be denied. They will have spending money as long as they live, and they will find an eternal heritage of glorious treasure when they enter into the joy of the Lord.

If all these things are to be had by merely knocking at mercy's door, Oh my soul, knock hard this morning, and ask large things of your generous Lord. Do not leave the throne of grace until all your wants have been spread before the Lord and until by faith you are persuaded that they will be supplied.

Do not be bashful when Jesus invites. No unbelief should hinder when Jesus promises. No cold heart should restrain when such blessings are to be obtained.

—from *Morning and Evening*

Alive in Christ

But God, who is rich in mercy, because of His great love with which He loved us, even when we were dead in trespasses, made us alive together with Christ (by grace you have been saved), and raised us up together, and made us sit together in the heavenly places in Christ Jesus, that in the ages to come He might show the exceeding riches of His grace in His kindness toward us in Christ Jesus.

For by grace you have been saved through faith, and that not of yourselves; it is the gift of God, not of works, lest anyone should boast. For we are His workmanship, created in Christ Jesus for good works, which God prepared beforehand that we should walk in them. . . .

Now, therefore, you are no longer strangers and foreigners, but fellow citizens with the saints and members of the household of God, having been built on the foundation of the apostles and prophets, Jesus Christ Himself being the chief cornerstone, in whom the whole building, being fitted together, grows into a holy temple in the Lord, in whom you also are being built together for a dwelling place of God in the Spirit.

A View of Grace

DANIEL DEFOE

July 4. In the morning I took the Bible, and beginning at the New Testament, I began seriously to read it, and imposed upon myself to read a while every morning and every night, not tying myself to the number of chapters, but as long as my thoughts should engage me. It was not long after I set seriously to this work, but I found my heart more deeply and sincerely affected with the wickedness of my past life. The impression of my dream revived, and the words, "All these things have not brought thee to repentance," ran seriously in my thought. I was earnestly begging of God to give me repentance, when it happened providentially the very day that, reading the Scripture, I came to these words, "He is exalted a Prince and a Saviour, to give repentance, and to give remission." I threw down the book, and with my heart as well as my hands lifted up to Heaven, in a kind of ecstasy of joy, I cried out aloud, "Jesus, thou son of David, Jesu, thou exalted Prince and Saviour, give me repentance!"

This was the first time that I could say, in the true sense of the words, that I prayed in all my life; for now I prayed with a sense of my condition, and with a true Scripture view of hope founded on the encouragement of the Word of God; and from this time, I may say, I began to have hope that God would hear me.

—from *Robinson Crusoe*

Rock of Ages

AUGUSTUS M. TOPLADY

Rock of Ages, cleft for me,
Let me hide myself in Thee;
Let the water and the blood,
From Thy wounded side which flowed,
Be of sin the double cure;
Save from wrath and make me pure.

Not the labor of my hands
Can fulfill Thy law's demands;
Could my zeal no respite know,
Could my tears forever flow,
All for sin could not atone;
Thou must save, and Thou alone.

Nothing in my hand I bring,
Simply to the cross I cling;
Naked, come to Thee for dress;
Helpless look to Thee for grace;
Foul, I to the fountain fly;
Wash me, Savior, or I die.

While I draw this fleeting breath,
When mine eyes shall close in death,
[*originally* When my eye-strings break in death,]
When I soar to worlds unknown,
See Thee on Thy judgment throne,
Rock of Ages, cleft for me,
Let me hide myself in Thee.

Relying on God's Grace

R. C. SPROUL

Perhaps the most difficult task for us to perform is to rely on God's grace and God's grace alone for our salvation. It is difficult for our pride to rest on grace. Grace is for other people—for beggars. We don't want to live by a heavenly welfare system. We want to earn our own way and atone for our own sins. We like to think we will go to heaven because we deserve to be there.

All the suffering I could possibly endure could not earn me a place in heaven. Nor can I merit the merit of Christ through suffering. I am altogether an unprofitable servant who must rely on someone else's merit to be saved.

With Paul we can rejoice in our sufferings if they enhance the glory of Christ. We can rejoice in our persecutions and look forward to the promised blessing of Christ. But the blessing Christ promised, the blessing of great reward, is a reward of grace. The blessing is promised even though it is not earned.

Augustine said it this way: "Our rewards in heaven are a result of God's crowning His own gifts. *Sola gratia.*"

—from *In the Presence of God*

Generous Grace

BRYAN CHAPELL

The message of unfair but generous grace is for us also. Often we resolve to be more holy, to give of ourselves more freely, to give up more of the world, and to follow our Savior wherever he leads. All too soon most of us find ourselves to be betrayers of those resolutions and of our Lord. We become those who subtract from the work of his kingdom and, in the context of our privileges and desires to do so much better, the repugnance of our sin can so sicken us that we despair of ever being acceptable to our God. In those moments of self-reproach, Jesus' account of the generous heart of a master's grace must echo in our souls.

Despite our early longings for justice, we find our ultimate comfort in the God who says through his Son, "Friend, do not be offended by your Master's generosity that you, too, need."

On the trip to Germany that I described earlier, we passed the site of the Buchenwald concentration camp of World War II. Our German bus guide began to reflect on what became one of his consistent themes throughout that section of our journey: his own dismay at the evil of his father's generation. He asked, "How could they have turned their heads from the evil of the concentration camps? How could they have allowed the Holocaust?"

He spoke of the patterns of the German officers who oversaw the grisly work of the death camps. "Like good German engineers," he said, "they would destroy precisely one thousand people because that was in the work orders for the day. They would not murder one more or one less person. Then, having committed this monstrosity, they would go home to bratwurst and beer, play with their children, listen to a recording of Shubert and, then, return the next day to murder precisely one thousand more."

The guide gave this version of the account with palpable anger in his voice and with the confession that, as a result of his deep disgust over these injustices of a previous generation, he had not spoken with his own father in years. Yet later on our journey, while observing the drug-pushers and promiscuous young people gathered outside our hotel in downtown Berlin, this same guide openly verbalized his wishes for a new government that would "get rid of the street riff-raff."

The sin of disregard for the sanctity of human life that he so hated in his father unconsciously resided in our guide himself. His resolve to do better and to be better than a previous generation could not eradicate the fissures of hatred and prejudice in his own heart.

Defects reside in every heart. Some are as hidden to our consciences as were our guide's to him, but others glare in our vision. When we see the dimensions of evil within each of us, and learn to suspect that there are others as yet unperceived, then we truly value our Savior's promise to be more than fair. We all need his assurance that he is rich in mercy. Such generosity in him secures our hope, creates our willingness to repent of our waywardness, inspires our desire to labor in his vineyard, and equips us to serve him with the joy that is our strength.

Our striving for good, longing for holiness, and resolving endlessly to do better than we are, while facing the daily reality of our lusts, our capacity for unbridled anger, our tendency to resent others for their abilities, and our inability to serve God without concern for our own interests, can tempt us to despair. However, when we remember that we serve the One who calls his betrayer "Friend" (Matt. 26:50), then we have new hope for bearing fruit in our lives and new incentive to labor for him.

The riches of God's mercy not only secure our way to him, they also provide our daily motivation and enablement to serve him. For this reason, our Master promises that he will be much more than fair. Our God will lavish us with his grace:

> [H]e does not treat us as our sins deserve
> or repay us according to our iniquities.
> For as high as the heavens are above the earth,
> so great is his love for those who fear him;
> as far as the east is from the west,
> so far has he removed our transgressions from us.
> As a father has compassion on his children,
> so the LORD has compassion on those who fear him;
> for he knows how we are formed,
> he remembers that we are dust. (Ps. 103:10–14 NIV)

—from *Holiness by Grace*

The Seal of Grace

MICHAEL GREEN

Finally, the Cross is a *pledge of total acceptance*. If I am honest about the failures in my own life, the evil I still do, the depths of wickedness to which I know I can and sometimes do still stoop, how can I be sure that God will still bother about me? After all, why should He? The answer lies in the cross of Jesus. Because He died there in actual and public agony, I know God will not go back on His contract with me, however much I mess up my end of it. The death of Jesus is the seal on the whole transaction. It is the marriage ring on the whole relationship. It is the adoption certificate into the family, the naturalization papers into the kingdom.

Whatever imagery you find helpful—this is the seal, this is the guarantee. So much that in John Bunyan's great classic *Pilgrim's Progress*, Christian's heavy burden fell off at the cross of Jesus and was seen no more, and he went on his way with freedom and joy. So much that the apostle Paul could exult, "There is therefore now no condemnation for those who are in Christ Jesus" (Rom. 8:1). None. My accusing guilt has been dealt with once and for all by what Jesus did for me on the cross. My acceptance in the family is assured not because of what I have done but because of what He has done. I shall never be thrown out for misconduct not because I deserve my membership but because He has guaranteed it. The warranty is written in His blood. Could any pledge be more trustworthy?

Sometimes when we encounter sheer generosity on a massive scale, we feel embarrassed. But at other times our eyes light up with

wonder, and we throw ourselves into the arms of our generous bene-
factor. This is what Jesus Christ wants us to do in response to His
breathtaking gift. The hymn writer put it well:

> Nothing in my hand I bring
> Simply to the cross I cling.

That is the only proper response to such a gift.

—from *Who Is This Jesus?*

The Fountain of Grace

DWIGHT L. MOODY

The first promise given to fallen man was a promise of grace. God never promised Adam anything when He put him in Eden. God never entered into a covenant with him as He did with Abraham. God told him, "Of the tree of the knowledge of good and evil, thou shalt not eat of it: for in the day that thou eatest thereof thou shalt surely die" (Gen. 2:17 KJV); but when this came to pass, then God came and gave him a gracious promise. He dealt in grace with him. As he left the Garden of Eden he could say to Eve, "Well, God does love us, though He has driven us out." There was no sign that Adam recognized his lost condition. As far as we know there was no cry for mercy or pardon, no confession of sin. Yet we find that God dealt in grace with him. God sought Adam out that He might bestow His grace upon him. He met Adam in his lost and ruined condition, and the first thing He did was to proclaim the promise of a coming Saviour.

For six thousand years, God has been trying to teach the world this great and glorious truth—that He wants to deal with man in love and in grace. It runs right through the Bible; all along you find this stream of grace flowing. The very last promise in the closing chapter of Revelation, like the first promise in Eden, is a promise of grace: "Whosoever will, let him take the water of life freely" (Rev. 22:17 KJV). So the whole revelation, and the whole history of man is encircled with grace, the free favor of God.

Some years ago when I was speaking on this subject, a friend sent me the following: "By the grace of God I am what I am!" This is the believer's eternal confession. Grace found him a rebel—it leaves him a son. Grace found him wandering at the gates of hell— it leads him through the gates of heaven. Grace devised the scheme of Redemption: Justice never would; Reason never could. And it is grace which carries out that scheme. No sinner would ever have sought his God "but by grace." The thickets of Eden would have proved Adam's grave, had not grace called him out. Saul would have lived and died the haughty self-righteous persecutor, had not grace laid him low. The thief would have continued breathing out his blasphemies, had not grace arrested his tongue and tuned it for glory.

"Out of the knottiest timber," says Rutherford, "He can make vessels of mercy for service in the high palace of glory."

"'I came, I saw, I conquered,'" says Toplady, "may be inscribed by the Saviour on every monument of grace. 'I came to the sinner; I looked upon him; and with a look of omnipotent love, I conquered.'"

"My friend, [Rutherford writes], we would have been this day wandering stars, to whom is reserved the blackness of darkness— Christless, hopeless, portionless—had not grace invited us, and grace constrained us."

—from *Sovereign Grace*

The Mover

O Supreme Moving Cause,

May I always be subordinate to Thee,

be dependent upon Thee,

be found in the path where Thou dost walk,

and where Thy Spirit moves,

take heed of estrangement from Thee,

of becoming insensible to Thy love.

Thou dost not move men like stones,

but dost endue them with life,

not to enable them to move without Thee,

but in submission to Thee, the first Mover.

O Lord, I am astonished at the difference

between my receivings and my deservings,

between the state I am now in and my past gracelessness,

between the heaven I am bound for and the hell I merit.

Who made me to differ, but Thee?

for I was no more ready to receive Christ than were others;

I could not have begun to love Thee hadst Thou not first loved me,

or been willing unless Thou hadst first made me so.

O that such a crown should fit the head of such a sinner!

such high advancement be for an unfruitful person!

such joys for so vile a rebel!

Infinite wisdom cast the design of salvation

into the mould of purchase and freedom;

Let *wrath deserved* be written on the door of hell,

But *the free gift of grace* on the gate of heaven.

I know that my sufferings are the result of my sinning,

but in heaven both shall cease;

Grant me to attain this haven and done with sailing,

and may the gales of Thy mercy blow me safely into the harbour.

Let Thy love draw me nearer to Thyself,

wean me from sin, mortify me to this world,

and make me ready for my departure hence.

Secure me by Thy grace as I sail across this stormy sea.

—from *The Valley of Vision:*
A Collection of Puritan Prayers and Devotions

Clothed with Christ

MAX LUCADO

For years I owned an elegant suit complete with coat, trousers, even a hat. I considered myself quite dapper in the outfit and was confident others agreed.

The pants were cut from the cloth of my good works, sturdy fabric of deeds done and projects completed. Some studies here, some sermons there. Many people complimented my trousers, and I confess, I tended to hitch them up in public so people would notice them.

The coat was equally impressive. It was woven together from my convictions. Each day I dressed myself in deep feelings of religious fervor. My emotions were quite strong. So strong, in fact, that I was often asked to model my cloak of zeal in public gatherings to inspire others. Of course I was happy to comply.

While there I'd also display my hat, a feathered cap of knowledge. Formed with my own hands from the fabric of personal opinion, I wore it proudly.

Surely God is impressed with my garments, I often thought. Occasionally I strutted into his presence so he could compliment the self-tailored wear. He never spoke. *His silence must mean admiration,* I convinced myself.

But then my wardrobe began to suffer. The fabric of my trousers grew thin. My best works started coming unstitched. I began leaving more undone than done, and what little I did was nothing to boast about.

No problem, I thought. *I'll work harder.*

But working harder *was* a problem. There was a hole in my coat of convictions. My resolve was threadbare. A cold wind cut into my chest. I reached up to pull my hat down firmly, and the brim ripped off in my hands.

Over a period of a few months, my wardrobe of self-righteousness completely unraveled. I went from tailored gentlemen's apparel to beggars' rags. Fearful that God might be angry at my tattered suit, I did my best to stitch it together and cover my mistakes. But the cloth was so worn. And the wind was so icy. I gave up. I went back to God. (Where else could I go?)

On a wintry Thursday afternoon, I stepped into his presence, not for applause, but for warmth. My prayer was feeble.

"I feel naked."

"You are. And you have been for a long time."

What he did next I'll never forget. "I have something to give you," he said. He gently removed the remaining threads and then picked up a robe, a regal robe, the clothing of his own goodness. He wrapped it around my shoulders. His words to me were tender. *"My son, you are now clothed with Christ"* (see Gal. 3:27).

Though I'd sung the hymn a thousand times, I finally understood it:

> *Dressed in his righteousness alone,*
> *faultless to stand before the throne.*[1]

—from the Introduction to *In the Grip of Grace*

By Grace Through Faith

CHARLES SPURGEON

By grace are ye saved through faith. (Eph. 2:8 KJV)

I think it well to turn a little to one side that I may ask my reader to observe adoringly the fountainhead of our salvation, which is the grace of God. "By grace are ye saved." Because God is gracious, therefore sinful men are forgiven, converted, purified, and saved. It is not because of anything in them, or that ever can be in them, that they are saved; but because of the boundless love, goodness, pity, compassion, mercy, and grace of God. Tarry a moment, then, at the well-head. Behold the pure river of water of life, as it proceeds out of the throne of God and of the Lamb! What an abyss is the grace of God! Who can measure its breadth? Who can fathom its depth? Like all the rest of the divine attributes, it is infinite. God is full of love, for "God is love." God is full of goodness; the very name "God" is short for "good." Unbounded goodness and love enter into the very essence of the Godhead. It is because "His mercy endureth forever" that men are not destroyed; because "His compassions fail not" that sinners are brought to Him and forgiven. Remember this; or you may fall into error by fixing your minds so much upon the faith which is the channel of salvation as to forget the grace which is the fountain and source even of faith itself. Faith is the work of God's grace in us. No man can say that Jesus is the Christ but by the Holy Ghost. "No man cometh unto me," saith Jesus, "except the Father which hath sent me draw him." So that faith, which is coming to Christ, is the result of divine drawing. Grace is the first and last moving cause of salvation; and faith, essential as it is, is only an important part of the machinery which grace employs. We are saved "through faith," but salvation is "by grace." Sound forth those words as with the archangel's trumpet: "By grace are ye saved." What glad tidings for the undeserving! Faith occupies the position of a channel or conduit pipe. Grace is the fountain and the stream; faith is the aqueduct along which the flood of mercy flows down to refresh the thirsty sons of men. It is a great pity when the aqueduct is broken. It is a sad sight to see around Rome the many noble aqueducts which no longer convey water into the city, because the arches are broken and the marvelous structures are in ruins. The aqueduct must be kept entire to convey the current; and, even so, faith must be true and sound, leading right up to God and coming right down to ourselves, that it may become a serviceable channel of mercy to our souls. Still, I again remind you that faith is only the channel or aqueduct, and not the fountainhead, and we must not look so much to it as to exalt it above the divine source of all blessing which lies in the grace of God. Never make a Christ out of your faith, nor think of it as if it were the independent source of your salvation. Our life is found in "looking unto Jesus," not in looking to our own faith. By faith all things become possible to us; yet the power is not in the faith, but in the God upon whom faith relies. Grace is the powerful engine, and faith is the chain by which the carriage of the soul is attached to the great motive power. The righteousness of faith is not the moral excellence of faith, but the righteousness of Jesus Christ which faith grasps and appropriates. The peace within the soul is not derived from the contemplation of our own faith; but it comes to us from Him who is our peace, the hem of whose garment faith touches, and virtue comes out of Him into the soul. See then, dear friend, that the weakness of your faith will not destroy you. A trembling hand may receive a golden gift. The Lord's salvation can come to us though we have only faith as a grain of mustard seed. The power lies in the grace of God, and not in our faith. Great messages can be sent along slender wires, and the peace-giving witness of the Holy Spirit can reach the heart by means of a thread-like faith which seems almost unable to sustain its own weight. Think more of Him to whom you look than of the look itself. You must look away even from your own looking, and see nothing but Jesus, and the grace of God revealed in Him.

—from *All of Grace*

Out of the Depths

MARTIN LUTHER

Out of the depths I cry to Thee,
Lord God! Oh hear my prayer!
Incline a gracious ear to me,
And bid me not despair.
If Thou rememberest each misdeed,
If each should have its rightful meed,
Lord, who shall stand before Thee?

'Tis through Thy love alone we gain
The pardon of our sin;
The strictest life is but in vain;
Our works can nothing win,
That none should boast himself of aught,
But own in fear Thy grace hath wrought
What in him seemeth righteous.

Wherefore my hope is in the Lord,
My works I count but dust.
I build not there but on His word,
And in His goodness trust.
Up to His care myself I yield;
He is my tower, my rock, my shield,
And for His help I tarry.

Though great our sins and sore our wounds
And deep dark our fall,
His helping mercy hath no bounds;
His love surpasseth all.
Our truly loving Shepherd He,
Who shall at last set Israel free
From all their sin and sorrow.

SUFFICIENT GRACE

My grace is sufficient for you,
for My strength is made perfect in weakness.

—2 CORINTHIANS 12:9

If and when a horror turns up
you will then be given Grace to help you.
I don't think one is usually given it in advance . . .
the little daily *support for the* daily *trial.*
Life has to be taken day by day and hour by hour.

—C. S. LEWIS

Grace Enough

GEORGE MACDONALD

But Thou art making me, I thank Thee, Sire.

What Thou hast done and doest Thou know'st well,

And I will help Thee: gently in Thy fire

I will lie burning; on Thy potter's-wheel

I will whirl patient, though my brain should reel.

Thy grace shall be enough the grief to quell,

And growing strength perfect through weakness dire.

—from *Diary of an Old Soul*

Come to the Throne of Grace

CYNTHIA HEALD

I don't know how many times in my life I have said, "Lord, I can't do this." Each time the Lord has patiently replied, *I know you can't, Cynthia. But I can through you.* And that is the mystery and the good news of the sufficiency of His grace in our lives. And it is the comfort of knowing that God delights in working through those who are weak, inadequate, and unworthy. For His strength is made perfect in our weakness, His Spirit is our adequacy, and Christ in us makes us worthy.

Paul gave Timothy the admonition, "You therefore, my son, be strong in the grace that is in Christ Jesus" (2 Tim. 2:1 NASB). Our strength is in His grace and His grace alone. It is not in our abilities, in our accomplishments past or present, in our successful service, or in our praise and emulation of others. To be strong in His grace, we must learn to take hold of it and appropriate it for our needs.

Hebrews 4:15–16 teaches us how to take hold of God's grace with this encouragement: "This High Priest of ours understands our weaknesses, for he faced all of the same temptations we do, yet he did not sin. So let us come boldly to the throne of our gracious God. There we will receive his mercy, and we will find grace to help us when we need it"(NLT).

To be strong in His grace, *we must come to the throne of grace.*

When Paul agonized over his thorn, he didn't go off in a corner to complain. He went to the Lord with his need and prayed for the thorn to be removed.

—from *A Woman's Journey to the Heart of God*

Grace Active

O God, may Thy Spirit speak in me that I may speak to Thee. O Lord Jesus, great high priest, Thou hast opened a new and living way by which a fallen creature can approach Thee with acceptance.

Help me to contemplate the dignity of Thy Person, the perfectness of Thy sacrifice, the effectiveness of Thy intercession.

O what blessedness accompanies devotion, when under all the trials that weary me, the cares that corrode me, the fears that disturb me, the infirmities that oppress me, I can come to Thee in my need and feel peace beyond understanding!

The grace that restores is necessary to preserve, lead, guard, supply, help me. And here Thy saints encourage my hope; they were once poor and are now rich, bound and are now free, tried and now are victorious.

Every new duty calls for more grace than I now possess, but not more than is found in Thee, the divine treasury in whom all fullness dwells. To Thee I repair for grace upon grace, until every void made by sin be replenished and I am filled with all Thy fullness.

May my desires be enlarged and my hopes emboldened, that I may honour Thee by my entire dependency and the greatness of my expectation.

Do Thou be with me, and prepare me for all the smiles of prosperity, the frowns of adversity, the losses of substance, the death of friends, the days of darkness, the changes of life, and the last great change of all. May I find Thy grace sufficient for all my needs.

—from *The Valley of Vision:*
A Collection of Puritan Prayers and Devotions

Timely and Needed Help

> *Let us therefore come boldly to the throne of grace, that we may obtain*
> *mercy, and find grace to help in time of need.*
>
> *—Hebrews 4:16*

Need! Time of need! Every hour we live is a time of need; and we are safest and happiest when we feel our needs most keenly. If you say that you are rich, and increased in goods, and have need of nothing, you are in the greatest destitution; but when you know yourself to be wretched, miserable, poor, blind, and naked, then the traveling merchantman is already standing on your doorstep, knocking (Rev. 3:17–20). It is when the supply runs short that Cana's King makes the vessels brim with wine. Have you been convinced of your need? If not, it is quite likely that you will live and die without a glimpse of the rich provision which God has made to meet it. Of what use is it to talk of rich provisions and sumptuous viands to those already satiated? But when the soul, by the straits of its necessity, has been brought to the verge of desperation, when we cry with the lepers of old, "If we say, 'We will enter the city,' the famine is in the city, and we shall die there. And if we sit here, we die also," then we are on the verge of discovering the rich provision that awaits us (2 Kings 7:8): all spiritual blessings in the heavenlies (Eph. 1:3); and all things that pertain to life and godliness (2 Pet. 1:3). There are two causes, therefore, why many Christians are living such impoverished

110 • AMAZED BY GRACE

lives: they have never realized their own infinite need; and they have never availed themselves of those infinite resources which hang within their reach, like fruit from the stooping boughs of an orchard in autumn.

Our needs are twofold. We need mercy. This is our fundamental need. Mercy when we are at our worst, yes, and at our best; mercy when the pruning knife cuts deep, yes, and when we are covered with foliage, flower, or fruit; mercy when we are broken and sore vexed, yes, and when we stand on the paved sapphire work upon the mountain summit to talk with God. The greatest saint among us can no more exist without the mercy of God than the ephemeral insects of a summer's noon can live without the sun.

We need grace to help. Help to walk through the valleys; and to walk on the high places, where the chamois can hardly stand. Help to suffer, to be still, to wait, to overcome, to make green one tiny spot of garden ground in God's great tillage. Help to live and to die. Each of these is met at the throne. Come, let us go to it. It is not the great white throne of judgment, but the rainbow-girt throne of grace. "No," you cry, "never! I am a man of unclean lips and heart; I dare not face Him before whom angels veil their faces; the fire of His awful purity will leap out on me, shriveling and consuming. I exceedingly fear and quake; or, if I muster courage enough to go once, I shall never be able to go as often as I need, or to ask for the common and trivial gifts required in daily living." Hush, soul! Thou mayest approach as often and as boldly as thou wilt; for we have a great High Priest, who is passed through the heavens, and not one who cannot be touched with the feeling of our infirmities.

A Priest. Deep down in the heart of men there is a strong and instinctive demand for a priest, to be daysman and mediator, to lay one hand on man and the other on God, and to go between them both. Wit and sarcasm may launch their epithets on this primordial craving; but they might as well try to extinguish by the same methods the craving of the body for food, of the understanding for truth, of the heart for love. And no religion is destined to meet the deepest yearnings of the race, which does not have glowing at the heart the provision of a priest to stand before the throne of grace; as, of old, the priest stood before the mercy seat, which was its literal prefigurement under the dispensation of the Levitical law. . . .

A Great High Priest. All other high priests were inferior to [Christ]. He is as much superior to the high priests as any one of them was to the priests of his time. But this does not exhaust His greatness. He does not belong to their line at all, but to an older, more venerable, and grander one; of which that mysterious personage was the founder, to whom Abraham, the father of Israel, gave tithes and homage. "Declared of God a High Priest after the order of Melchizedek." Nay, further, His greatness is that of the Son of God, the fellow and equal of Deity. He is as great as His infinite nature and the divine appointment and His ideal of ministry could make Him.

Passed through the heavens. Between the holy place where the priest daily performed the service of the sanctuary, and the inner shrine forbidden to all save to the high priest once each year, there hung a veil of blue. And of what was that blue veil the emblem, save of those heavenly curtains, the work of God's fingers, which hang between our mortal vision and the marvels of his presence chamber? Once a year the high priest carried the blood of propitiation through the blue veil of separation, and sprinkled it upon the mercy seat; and in this significant and solemn act he typified the entrance of our blessed Lord into the immediate presence of God, bearing the marks and emblems of His atoning death, and taking up His position there as our Mediator and Intercessor, in whom we are represented, and for whose sake we are accepted and beloved.

Touched with the feeling of our infirmities. He hates the sin, but loves the sinner. His hatred to the one is measured by His cross; His love to the other is as infinite as His nature. And His love is not a dreamy ecstasy; but practical, because all the machinery of temptation was brought into operation against Him. It would take too long to enumerate the points at which the great adversary of souls assails us; but there is not a sense, a faculty, a power, which may not be the avenue of His attack. Through eye-gate, ear-gate, and thought-gate His squadrons seek to pour. And, marvelous though it be, yet our High Priest was tempted in all these points, in body, soul, and spirit; though there was no faltering in His holy resolution, no vacillation or shadow of turning, no desire to yield. "The prince of this world cometh, and hath nothing in me."

All His experiences are vividly present to Him still; and whenever we go to Him, pleading for mercy or help, He instantly knows just how much and where we need it, and immediately His intercessions obtain for us, and His hands bestow, the exact form of either we may require. "He is touched." That sympathetic heart is the metropolis to which each afferent nerve carries an immediate thrill from the meanest and remotest members of His body, bringing at once in return the very help and grace which are required. Oh to live in touch with Christ! always touching Him, as of old the woman touched His garment's hem; and receiving responses, quick as the lightning flash, and full of the healing, saving virtue of God (Mark 5:28).

—from *The Way into the Holiest*

My Shepherd Will Supply My Need

ISAAC WATTS

My Shepherd will supply my need,
The God of love supreme;
In pastures green you make me feed,
Beside the living stream.

You bring my wand'ring spirit back,
When I forsake your ways;
And lead me for your mercy's sake,
In paths of truth and grace.

When I walk through the shades of death,
Your presence is my stay;
One word of your supporting breath
Drives all my fears away.

Your hand, in sight of all my foes,
Does still my table spread;
My cup with blessings overflows;
Your oil anoints my head.

The sure provisions of my God
Attend me all my days;
Oh, may your house be my abode,
And all my work be praise!

There would I find a settled rest,
While others go and come;
No more a stranger or a guest,
But like a child at home.

In Boldness I Come

JOHN CHRYSOSTOM

I am not worthy, Master and Lord, that Thou shouldst come beneath the roof of my soul: yet since Thou in Thy love toward all men, dost wish to dwell in me, in boldness I come.

Thou commandest, open the gates—which Thou alone hast forged. And Thou wilt come in with love toward all men, as is Thy nature; Thou wilt come in and enlighten my darkened reasoning.

I believe that Thou wilt do this: for Thou didst not send away the harlot who came to Thee with tears; nor cast out the repenting publican; nor reject the thief who acknowledged Thy kingdom; nor forsake the repentant persecutor, a yet greater act. But all those who came to Thee in repentance didst Thou count in the band of Thy friends, who alone abidest blessed forever, now, and until the endless ages.

From Every Stormy Wind

HUGH STOWELL

From every stormy wind that blows,
From every swelling tide of woes,
There is a calm, a sure retreat;
'Tis found beneath the mercy seat.

There is a place where Jesus sheds
The oil of gladness on our heads;
A place than all besides more sweet;
It is the blood-bought mercy seat.

There is a scene where spirits blend,
Where friend holds fellowship with friend;
Though sundered far, by faith they meet
Around one common mercy seat.

There, there, on eagles' wings we soar,
And time and sense seem all no more;
And heaven comes down, our souls to greet,
And glory crowns the mercy seat.

Oh, let my hand forget her skill,
My tongue be silent, cold, and still,
This bounding heart forget to beat,
If I forget the mercy seat!

—from *The Winter's Wreath,*
a Collection of Original Contributions in Prose and Verse

Grace upon Grace

Test yourself with this question: What if God's only gift to you were his grace to save you. Would you be content? You beg him to save the life of your child. You plead with him to keep your business afloat. You implore him to remove the cancer from your body. What if his answer is, "My grace is enough." Would you be content?

You see, from heaven's perspective, grace is enough. If God did nothing more than save us from hell, could anyone complain? . . . Having been given eternal life, dare we grumble at an aching body? Having been given heavenly riches, dare we bemoan earthly poverty? . . .

If you have eyes to read these words, hands to hold this book, the means to own this volume, he has already given you grace upon grace.

—from *In the Grip of Grace*

120 • AMAZED BY GRACE

There's a Wideness in God's Mercy

FREDERICK WILLIAM FABER

There's a wideness in God's mercy
Like the wideness of the sea;
There's a kindness in His justice,
Which is more than liberty.
There is welcome for the sinner
And more graces for the good;
There is mercy with the Saviour;
There is healing in His blood.

There is no place where earth's sorrows
Are more felt than up in heaven;
There is no place where earth's failings
Have such kindly judgement given.
There is plentiful redemption
In the blood that has been shed;
There is joy for all the members
In the sorrows of the Head.

For the love of God is broader
Than the measure of man's mind;
And the heart of the Eternal
Is most infinitely kind.
If our love were but more simple,
We should take Him at His word;
And our lives would be all sunshine
In the sweetness of the Lord.

Restraining Grace

SAMUEL RUTHERFORD

It is grace which, at this moment, keeps us. We have often been a Peter—forsaking our Lord, but brought back to Him again. Why not a Demas or a Judas? "I have prayed for thee, that thy faith fail not." Is not this our own comment and reflection on life's retrospect? "Yet not I, but the grace of God which was with me."

Oh, let us seek to realize our continual dependence on this grace every moment! "More grace! more grace!" should be our continual cry. But the infinite supply is commensurate with the infinite need. The treasury of grace, though always emptying is always full: the key of prayer which opens it is always at hand: and the almighty [Giver] of the blessings of grace is always waiting to be gracious. The recorded promise never can be canceled or reversed—"My grace is sufficient for thee" (2 Cor. 12:9 KJV).

Let us seek to dwell much on this inexhaustible theme. The grace of God is the source of minor temporal as well as of higher spiritual blessings.

It accounts for the crumb of daily bread as well as for the crown of eternal glory. But even in regard to earthly mercies, never forget the channel of grace through Christ Jesus. It is sweet thus to connect every (even the smallest and humblest) token of providential bounty with Calvary's Cross—to have the common blessings of life stamped with the print of the nails; it makes them doubly precious to think this flows from Jesus. Let others be contented with the uncovenanted mercies of God. Be it ours to say as the children of grace and heirs of glory: "Our Father which art in heaven, give us this day our daily bread." Nay, reposing in the all-sufficiency in all things, promised by "the God of all grace."

A Hymn to God the Father

JOHN DONNE

Wilt Thou forgive that sin where I begun,
Which was my sin, though it were done before?
Wilt Thou forgive that sin, through which I run,
And do run still, though still I do deplore?
When Thou hast done, Thou hast not done,
For I have more.

Wilt Thou forgive that sin which I have won
Others to sin, and made my sin their door?
Wilt Thou forgive that sin which I did shun
A year or two, but wallow'd in, a score?
When Thou hast done, Thou hast not done,
For I have more.

I have a sin of fear, that when I have spun
My last thread, I shall perish on the shore;
But swear by Thyself, that at my death Thy Son
Shall shine as He shines now, and heretofore;
And, having done that, Thou hast done;
I fear no more.

Grace for Living

Dwight L. Moody

What we want, more than anything else, is more grace in our lives, in our business affairs, in our homes, in our daily walk and conversation. I cannot but believe that the reason of the standard of Christian life being so low, is that we are living on stale manna. You know what I mean by that. So many people are living on their past experience—thinking of the grand times they had twenty years ago, perhaps when they were converted. It is a sure sign that we are out of communion with God if we are talking more of the joy, and peace, and power, we had in the past, than of what we have today. We are told to "grow in grace"; but a great many are growing the wrong way.

You remember the Israelites used to gather the manna fresh every day: they were not allowed to store it up. There is a lesson here for us Christians. If we would be strong and vigorous, we must go to God daily and get grace. A man can no more take in a supply of grace for the future than he can eat enough today to last him for the next six months; or take sufficient air into his lungs at once to sustain life for a week to come. We must draw upon God's boundless stores of grace from day to day, as we need it.

I knew a man who lived on the banks of Lake Erie. He had pipes laid to his house from the lake; and when he wanted water, all he had to do was to turn the tap and the water flowed in. If the government had presented him with the lake, he would not have known what to do with it. So we may say that if God were to give us grace enough for a lifetime, we should not know how to use it. He has given us the privilege of drawing on Him day by day—not "forty days after sight." There is plenty of grace in the bank of heaven; we need not be afraid of its becoming exhausted.

We are asked to come *boldly* to the throne of grace—as sons to a father—that we may find grace. You have noticed that a son is very much more bold in his father's house than if he were simply a servant. A good many Christians are like servants. If you go into a house, you can soon tell the difference between the family and the servants. A son comes home in the evening; he goes all over the house—perhaps talks about the letters that have come in, and wants to know all that has been going on in the family during his absence. It is very different with a servant, who perhaps does not leave the kitchen or the servants' hall all day except when duty requires it.

Suppose someone had paid a million dollars into the bank in your name and had given you a checkbook so that you could draw out just as you wanted: would you go to work and try to live on ten dollars a month? Yet that is exactly what many of us are doing as Christians. I believe this low standard of Christian life in the Church is doing more to manufacture infidels than all the skeptical books that were ever written.

Hear what the Apostle says: "My God shall supply *all* your need." Look at these words carefully. It does not say He will supply all your *wants*. There are many things we want that God has not promised to give. It is "your *need*" *and* "*all* your need." My children often want many things they do not get; but I supply all they need, if it is in my power to give it to them. I do not supply all their wants by any means. My boy would probably want to have me give him a horse; when I know that what he really needs, perhaps, is grace to control his temper. Our children might want many things that it would be injurious for them to have. And so, though God may withhold from us many things that we desire, He will supply all our need. There can come upon us no trouble or trial in this life, but God has grace enough to carry us right through it, if we will only go to Him and get it. But we must ask for it day by day. "As thy days, so shall thy strength be. . . ."

There is a story in the history of Elisha the prophet that I am very fond of; most of you are familiar with it. Sometimes we meet with people who hesitate to accept Christ, because they are so afraid they will not hold out. You remember there was a young prophet who died and left a widow with two little boys. It has been said that misfortunes do not come singly, but in battalions. This woman had not only lost her husband, but a creditor was going to take her boys and sell them into slavery. That was a common thing in those days. The widow went and told Elisha all about it. He asked her what she had in the house. Nothing, she said, but a pot of oil. It was a very hard case.

Elisha told her to go home and borrow all the vessels she could. His command was: "Borrow not a few." I like that. She took him at his word, and borrowed all the vessels her neighbors would lend to her. I can imagine I see the woman and her two sons going from house to house asking the loan of their vessels. No doubt there were a good many of the neighbors who were stretching their necks, and wondering what it all meant; just as we sometimes find people coming into the inquiry-room to see what is going on. If this woman had been like some modern skeptics, she would have thought it very absurd for the prophet to bid her do such a thing; she would have asked what good could come of it. But faith asks no questions: so she went and did what the man of God told her to do. I can see her going up one side of the street knocking at every door and asking for empty vessels. "How many do you want?" "All you can spare." There are the two sons carrying the great vessels; some of them perhaps nearly as large as the boys themselves. It was hard work. When they had finished one side of the street, they went down the other. "Borrow not a few," she had been told; so she went on asking for as many as she could get. If there were as much gossip in those days as there is now, all the people in the street would have been talking about her. Why, this woman and her boys have been carrying vessels into the house all day; what can be the matter?

But now they have all the vessels the neighbors would lend. She locks the door; and she says to one of the boys, "James, you are the younger; bring me the empty vessels. John, you are the stronger; when I have filled them you take them away." So she began to pour. Perhaps the first vessel was twice as big as the one she poured from; but it was soon filled: and she kept on pouring into vessel after vessel. At last her son says, "Mother, this is the last one"; and we are told that the oil was not stayed till the last vessel was full.

Dear friends, bring your empty vessels; and God will fill them. I venture to say that the eyes of those boys sparkled as they saw this beautiful oil, fresh from the hand of the Creator. The woman went and told the man of God what had happened; he said to her, "Go, sell the oil, and pay thy debt; and live thou and thy children off the rest." That is grace for the present and for the future. "As thy days, so shall thy strength be." You will have grace not only to cover all your sins, but to carry you right into glory. Let the grace of God into your heart; and He will bring you safely through.

—from *Sovereign Grace*

Do Thou for Me

AMY CARMICHAEL

Do Thou for Me, O God the Lord,
Do Thou for me.
I need not toil to find the word
That carefully
Unfolds my prayer and offers it,
My God, to Thee.

It is enough that Thou wilt do,
And wilt not tire,
Wilt lead by cloud, all the night through
By light of fire,
Till Thou hast perfected in me
Thy heart's desire.

For my beloved I will not fear,
Love knows to do
For him, for her, from year to year,
As hitherto.
Whom my heart cherishes are dear
To Thy heart too.

O blessed be the love that bears
The burden now,
The love that frames our very prayers,
Well knowing how
To coin our gold. O God the Lord,
Do Thou, do Thou.

—from *Toward Jerusalem*

The Death of Sin

ROMANS 6:8–11, 14; 11:6

Now if we died with Christ, we believe that we shall also live with Him, knowing that Christ, having been raised from the dead, dies no more. Death no longer has dominion over Him. For the death that He died, He died to sin once for all; but the life that He lives, He lives to God.

Likewise you also, reckon yourselves to be dead indeed to sin, but alive to God in Christ Jesus our Lord. . . .

For sin shall not have dominion over you, for you are not under law but under grace. . . .

And if by grace, then it is no longer of works; otherwise grace is no longer grace. But if it is of works, it is no longer grace; otherwise work is no longer work.

Approach, My Soul, the Mercy Seat

JOHN NEWTON

Approach, my soul, the mercy seat,
Where Jesus answers prayer;
There humbly fall before His feet,
For none can perish there.

Thy promise is my only plea,
With this I venture nigh;
Thou callest burdened souls to Thee,
And such, O Lord, am I.

Bowed down beneath a load of sin,
By Satan sorely pressed,
By war without and fears within,
I come to Thee for rest.

Be Thou my Shield and hiding Place,
That, sheltered by Thy side,
I may my fierce accuser face,
And tell him Thou hast died!

O wondrous love! to bleed and die,

To bear the cross and shame,

That guilty sinners, such as I,

Might plead Thy gracious Name.

"Poor tempest tossed soul, be still;

My promised grace receive";

'Tis Jesus speaks—I must, I will,

I can, I do believe.

—from *Olney Hymns*

But for the Grace of God

MARTIN LUTHER

The Law is a mirror to show a person what he is like, a sinner who is guilty of death, and worthy of everlasting punishment. What is this bruising and beating by the hand of the Law to accomplish? This, that we may find the way to grace. The Law is an usher to lead the way to grace. God is the God of the humble, the miserable, the afflicted. It is His nature to exalt the humble, to comfort the sorrowing, to heal the brokenhearted, to justify the sinners, and to save the condemned. The fatuous idea that a person can be holy by himself denies God the pleasure of saving sinners. God must therefore first take the sledgehammer of the Law in His fists and smash the beast of self-righteousness and its brood of self-confidence, self-wisdom, self-righteousness, and self-help.

When the conscience has been thoroughly frightened by the Law it welcomes the Gospel of grace with its message of a Savior who came into the world, not to break the bruised reed, nor to quench the smoking flax, but to preach glad tidings to the poor, to heal the brokenhearted, and to grant forgiveness of sins to all the captives.

Man's folly, however, is so prodigious that instead of embracing the message of grace with its guarantee of the forgiveness of sin for Christ's sake, man finds himself more laws to satisfy his conscience. "If I live," says he, "I will mend my life. I will do this, I will do that." Man, if you don't do the very opposite, if you don't send Moses with the Law back to Mount Sinai and take the hand of Christ, pierced for your sins, you will never be saved.

When the Law drives you to the point of despair, let it drive you a little farther, let it drive you straight into the arms of Jesus who says: "Come unto me, all ye that labour and are heavy laden, and I will give you rest." . . .

As certain as we are that Christ pleases God, so sure ought we to be that we also please God, because Christ is in us. And although we daily offend God by our sins, yet as often as we sin, God's mercy bends over us. Therefore sin cannot get us to doubt the grace of God. Our certainty is of Christ, that mighty Hero who overcame the Law, sin, death, and all evils. So long as He sits at the right hand of God to intercede for us, we have nothing to fear from the anger of God.

—from *Commentary on Galatians*

He Giveth More Grace

ANNIE JOHNSON FLINT

He giveth more grace when the burdens grow greater,
He sendeth more strength when the labors increase;
To added affliction He addeth His mercy,
To multiplied trials, His multiplied peace.

When we have exhausted our store of endurance,
When our strength has failed ere the day is half done,
When we reach the end of our hoarded resources,
Our Father's full giving is only begun.

His love has no limit, His grace has no measure,
His power no boundary known unto men;
For out of His infinite riches in Jesus
He giveth and giveth and giveth again.

GRACE
THAT
TRANSFORMS

But by the grace of God I am what I am,
and His grace toward me was not in vain.

—1 CORINTHIANS 15:10

Grace is indeed needed to turn a man into a saint;
and he who doubts it does not know what a saint or a man is.

—BLAISE PASCAL

The Grace Which Costs

DIETRICH BONHOEFFER

Cheap grace is the deadly enemy of our Church. We are fighting today for costly grace.

Cheap grace means grace sold on the market like cheapjacks' wares. The sacraments, the forgiveness of sin, and the consolations of religion are thrown away at cut prices. Grace is represented as the Church's inexhaustible treasury, from which she showers blessings with generous hands, without asking questions or fixing limits. Grace without price; grace without cost! The essence of grace, we suppose, is that the account has been paid in advance; and, because it has been paid, everything can be had for nothing. Since the cost was infinite, the possibilities of using and spending it are infinite. What would grace be if it were not cheap?

Cheap grace means grace as a doctrine, a principle, a system. It means forgiveness of sins proclaimed as a general truth, the love of God taught as the Christian "conception" of God. An intellectual assent to that idea is held to be of itself sufficient to secure remission of sins. The Church which holds the correct doctrine of grace has, it is supposed, *ipso facto* a part in that grace. In such a Church the world finds a cheap covering for its sins; no contrition is required, still less any real desire to be delivered from sin. Cheap grace therefore amounts to a denial of the Incarnation of the Word of God.

Cheap grace means the justification of sin without the justification of the sinner. Grace alone does everything, they say, and so everything can remain as it was before. "All for sin could not atone." The world goes on in the same old way, and we are still sinners "even in the best life" as Luther said. Well, then, let the Christian live like the rest of the world, let him model himself on the world's standards in every sphere of life, and not presumptuously aspire to live a different life under grace from his old life of sin. . . . Instead of following Christ, let the Christian enjoy the consolations of his grace! That is what we mean by cheap grace, the grace which amounts to the justification of the sin without the justification of the repentant sinner who departs from sin and from whom sin departs. Cheap grace is not the kind of forgiveness of sin which frees us from the toils of sin. Cheap grace is the grace we bestow on ourselves.

Cheap grace is the preaching of forgiveness without requiring repentance, baptism without church discipline, communion without confession, absolution without personal confession. Cheap grace is grace without discipleship, grace without the cross, grace without Jesus Christ, living and incarnate.

Costly grace is the treasure hidden in the field; for the sake of it a man will gladly go and sell all that he has. It is the pearl of great price to buy which the merchant will sell all his goods. It is the kingly rule of Christ, for whose sake a man will pluck out the eye which causes him to stumble, it is the call of Jesus Christ at which the disciple leaves his nets and follows him.

Costly grace is the gospel which must be *sought* again and again, the gift which must be *asked* for, the door at which a man must *knock*.

Such grace is *costly* because it calls us to follow, and it is *grace* because it calls us to follow *Jesus Christ*. It is costly because it costs a man his life, and it is grace because it gives a man the only true life. It is costly because it condemns sin, and grace because it justifies the sinner. Above all, it is *costly* because it cost God the life of his Son: "ye were bought at a price," and what has cost God much cannot be cheap for us. Above all it is *grace* because God did not reckon his Son too dear a price to pay for our life, but delivered him up for us. Costly grace is the Incarnation of God.

Costly grace is the sanctuary of God; it has to be protected from the world, and not thrown to the dogs. It is therefore the living word, the Word of God, which he speaks as it pleases him. Costly grace confronts us as a gracious call to follow Jesus, it comes as a word of forgiveness to the broken spirit and the contrite heart. Grace is costly because it compels a man to submit to the yoke of Christ and follow him; it is grace because Jesus says: "My yoke is easy and my burden is light."

—from *The Cost of Discipleship*

Will God Forgive What I'm About to Do?

Steven Spielberg's film version of *The Color Purple* includes a moving portrayal of a parable of grace. Sugar, a sexy, knock-'em-dead nightclub singer who works out of a ramshackle bar by the side of a river, is the classic prodigal daughter. Her father, a minister who preaches hellfire and brimstone in a church just across the way, hasn't spoken to her in years.

One day as Sug is crooning "I've got somethin' to tell you" in the bar, she hears the church choir answer, as if antiphonally, "God's got something to tell you!" Pricked by nostalgia or guilt, Sug leads her band to the church and marches down the aisle just as her father mounts the pulpit to preach on the prodigal son.

The sight of his long-lost daughter silences the minister, and he glowers at the procession coming down the aisle. "Even us sinners have soul," Sug explains, and hugs her father, who hardly reacts. Ever the moralist, he cannot easily forgive a daughter who has shamed him so.

The Hollywood portrayal, however, altogether misses the main point of the biblical parable. In Jesus' version the father does not glower, but rather searches the horizon, desperate for any sign of his wayward child. It is the father who runs, throws his arm around the prodigal, and kisses him.

By making a sinner the magnanimous hero, Hollywood dodges the scandal of grace. In truth what blocks forgiveness is not God's

144 • AMAZED BY GRACE

reticence—"But while he was still a long way off, his father saw him and was filled with compassion for him"—but ours. God's arms are always extended; we are the ones who turn away. It is a wonderful truth, and one subject to devious exploitation.

Not long ago I sat in a restaurant and listened to yet another variation on a familiar theme. Daniel confided that he had decided to leave his wife after fifteen years of marriage. He had met someone younger and prettier, he said, someone who "makes me feel alive, like I haven't felt in years."

Daniel, a Christian, knew well the personal and moral consequences of what he was about to do. His decision to leave would inflict permanent damage on his wife and three children. Even so, he said, the force pulling him toward the younger woman was too strong to resist.

I listened to his story with sadness and grief. Then, during the dessert course, he dropped the bombshell, "The reason I wanted to see you tonight was to ask you a question. Do you think God can forgive something as awful as I am about to do?"

Historian and art critic Robert Hughes tells of a convict sentenced to life imprisonment on a maximum security island off the coast of Australia. One day with no provocation he turned on a fellow prisoner he barely knew and beat him senseless. The murderer was shipped back to the mainland to stand trial, where he gave a straightforward, passionless account of the crime, showing no sign of remorse. "Why?" asked the bewildered judge. "What was your motive?"

The prisoner replied that he was sick of life on the island, a notoriously brutal place, and that he saw no reason to keep on living. "Yes,

yes, I understand all that," said the judge. "I can see why you might drown yourself in the ocean. But why murder?"

"Well, it's like this," said the prisoner. "I'm a Catholic. If I commit suicide I'll go straight to hell. But if I murder I can come back here and confess to a priest before my execution. That way, God will forgive me."

Do we fully appreciate the scandal of unconditional grace? How can I dissuade my friend Daniel from committing a terrible mistake if he knows forgiveness lies just around the corner? Or, worse, why not murder, like the Australian prisoner, if you know in advance you'll be forgiven?

The scandal of grace must have haunted the apostle Paul as he wrote the book of Romans. The first three chapters ring down condemnation on every class of human being, concluding, "There is no one righteous, not even one." The next two chapters unveil the miracle of a grace so boundless that, as Paul says, "where sin increased, grace increased all the more."

Paul's tone changes in chapter 6. I can almost see the apostle staring at the papyrus and scratching his head, thinking to himself, *Wait a minute! What have I said?* What's to keep a murderer, adulterer, or common sinner from exploiting God's lavish promise of "forgiveness in advance"?

More than once in the next few chapters Paul returns to this logical predicament: "What shall we say, then? Shall we go on sinning so that grace may increase?" To such a devious question he has a pithy answer ("By no means!" or, as the King James Version has it, "God forbid!") and a lengthy one. What Paul keeps circling around in those dense, wonderful chapters (6–8) is, quite simply, the scandal of grace.

Here is what I told my friend Daniel, in a nutshell. "Can God forgive you? Of course. Read your Bible. David, Peter, Paul—God builds his church on the backs of people who murder, commit adultery, deny him, and persecute his followers. But because of Christ, forgiveness is now our problem, not God's. What we have to go through to commit sin distances us from God—we change in the very act of rebellion—and there is no guarantee we will come back. You ask me about forgiveness now, but will you even want it later, especially if it involves repentance?"

Several months after our conversation, Daniel made his choice. I have yet to see any evidence of repentance. Now he tends to rationalize his decision as a way of escaping an unhappy marriage. He has rejected most of his Christian friends—"Too narrow-minded," he says—and looks instead for people who celebrate his newfound liberation.

To me, though, Daniel does not seem very liberated. The price of his "freedom" has meant turning his back on those who cared about him most. He also tells me God is not a part of his life right now. "Maybe later," he says.

God took a great risk by announcing forgiveness in advance. It occurs to me, though, that the scandal of grace involves a transfer of that risk to us. As George MacDonald put it, we are condemned not for the wicked things we've done, but for not leaving them.

—from *Finding God in Unexpected Places*

Grace Reigning

SCOTTY SMITH

One of the evidences of God's grace advancing reign in our lives is gospel vision—the gift of seeing behind the scenes to what is sometimes imperceptible for many years, the ability to gain perspective on hard-to-understand providences that seem incongruent with a God who is both good and in control.

Grace is reigning when we are able to say with Joseph—in the face of perplexing conundrums and cruel crises—"You intended to harm me, but God intended it for good to accomplish what is now being done, the saving of many lives" (Gen. 50:20 NIV). Grace is reigning when we seize, or are seized by, Paul's bold exclamation of faith—"And we know that in *all* things God works for the good of those who love him" (Rom. 8:28 NIV). Grace reigns when we start processing the inclusive claims of the "all" in "all things"—one by one. And grace reigns when we can look back over the chapters, paragraphs, and sentences of our complex stories and sing with tears of growing assurance, "Great is thy faithfulness, O God, my Father . . . great is thy faithfulness!"

—from *The Reign of Grace*

Come, Thou Fount of Every Blessing

ROBERT ROBINSON

Come, Thou Fount of every blessing,
Tune my heart to sing Thy grace;
Streams of mercy, never ceasing,
Call for songs of loudest praise.
Teach me some melodious sonnet,
Sung by flaming tongues above.
Praise the mount! I'm fixed upon it,
Mount of Thy redeeming love.

Here I raise my Ebenezer;
Here by Thy great help I've come;
And I hope, by Thy good pleasure,
Safely to arrive at home.
Jesus sought me when a stranger,
Wandering from the fold of God;
He, to rescue me from danger,
Interposed His precious blood.

O to grace how great a debtor
Daily I'm constrained to be!
Let Thy goodness, like a fetter,
Bind my wandering heart to Thee.
Prone to wander, Lord, I feel it,
Prone to leave the God I love;
Here's my heart, O take and seal it,
Seal it for Thy courts above.

O that day when freed from sinning,
I shall see Thy lovely face;
Clothed then in blood washed linen
How I'll sing Thy sovereign grace;
Come, my Lord, no longer tarry,
Take my ransomed soul away;
Send thine angels now to carry
Me to realms of endless day.

The Most Amazing Grace

Os Guinness

Bernard Mandeville wrote in *The Fable of the Bees* (1714) that "pride and vanity have built more hospitals than all the virtues together." It doesn't take a cynic to believe that pride and vanity have also painted paintings, composed music, written novels, dispensed fortunes, given extravagant gifts—and built cathedrals. . . .

The greatest artistic creators may be especially prone to this conceit. Creators, like God, they come to see themselves as challengers to God. D. H. Lawrence felt it in himself: "I always feel as if I stood naked for the fire of the Almighty to go through me—and it's rather an awful feeling. One has to be terribly religious, to be an artist." Critic George Steiner glimpses it in the "awesome encounters between God and the more god-like of his creatures. To have carved the figures in the Medici Chapel, to have imagined Hamlet and Falstaff, to have heard the *Missi Solemnis* out of deafness is to have said, in some mortal but irreducible manner: 'Let there be light.' It is to have wrestled with the angel." . . . Pride has traditionally been viewed as the first, worst, and deadliest of the seven deadly sins. But the contemporary world has tried to transform this vice into a virtue—through changing the definition of pride to self-respect. So pride no longer "goeth before a fall," it cometh before a promotion, provided you have sufficient self-confidence and self-esteem. "Pride has always been one of my favorite virtues," actress Dame Edith Sitwell wrote. "I have never regarded it, except in certain cases, as a major sin. . . . I despise anything which reduces the pride of Man."

But the deadly sin is not pride in the sense of self-respect, a justifiable sense of one's own worth. The sin of pride is wrong because it is inordinate and overweening. Consider its synonyms: egotism, arrogance, hubris, selfishness, vanity, haughtiness, presumption, boastfulness, big-headedness, self-satisfaction, self-centeredness, and the like. None of them is admirable and neither is the conceit that is the rotten fruit of calling. "The greatest curse in the spiritual life," Oswald Chambers wrote, "is conceit."

Notice how conceit twists calling in two separate ways. First, people who are called are especially vulnerable to pride because of the very nobility of the calling. Temptation is always the tempter's compliment to the tempted, so the strongest temptations are the subtlest. Put differently, temptation tempts most temptingly when it is a shortcut to realizing the very highest at which we aim. So the twisting of our highest aspirations will be twice as evil as the twisting of our lowest. Dorothy Sayer's warning applies to calling: "The devilish strategy of Pride is that it attacks us, not in our weakest points, but in our strongest. It is preeminently the sin of the noble mind."

Second, we who are called are vulnerable to a special form of pride because of our desire to wean ourselves from human audiences and live before the Audience of One. The trouble comes, of course, when we truly live before an Audience of One, but the audience is not God but us. As C. S. Lewis observed in *Mere Christianity*, that is why vanity is the least bad and most pardonable form of pride— the vain person is always angling for praise and admiration, living before the Audience of Thousands. In contrast, "The real black, diabolical Pride comes when you look down on others so much that you do not care what they think of you." The outcome, as the prophet Ezekiel wrote of the proud city of Tyre, is the point when we say, "I and who but I?" Or, as it was said of Charlie Chaplin's tyrannical and conceited meanness as a film director, it was all "me, me alone, and that's enough." . . .

Do we feel the wonder of being called? It is all a gift and all of grace. And contrary to expectations, grace is not a matter of God's welcoming the lawbreaker as well as the law-abiding, the disreputable along with the respectable, the prodigal son as well as the stay-at-home.

Quite the reverse. Pride is the first and worst sin, so grace is the most amazing when it embraces the fruits of pride rather than the fruits of gluttony or lust, when it reaches the Pharisee soul rather than the profligate Mary Magdalene, when it wins the proud person made prouder still by calling rather than the sinner feeling unworthy to be addressed.

Only grace can dissolve the hard, solitary, vaunting "I" of the sin of pride in each of us. But the good news is that it does.

—from *The Call*

Leave Your Life of Sin

JAMES MONTGOMERY BOICE

We must never think that grace, as wonderful as it is, either permits or encourages us to go on sinning. For it is not only "grace" that came through Jesus Christ. "Truth" did also (John 1:17). And the truth in this matter is that God still requires holiness of his people. "Shall we go on sinning so that grace may increase?" asked Paul. He answered, "By no means! We died to sin; how can we live in it any longer?" (Rom. 6:1–2 NIV).

This is why the ending of the story of Jesus and the woman trapped in adultery is so important, though it is often overlooked. Jesus did not only forgive her on the basis of his coming death for sin. True, he did forgive her. But having done that, he added, "Go and leave your life of sin." This always follows upon forgiveness. For God is unchanging, and he continues to be righteous and demand righteousness even when he is forgiving. No one can be saved and then continue to do as he or she pleases. If we are saved, we must stop sinning.

At the same time, we can be grateful that Jesus spoke as he did. For we notice that he did not say, "Leave your life of sin, and I will not condemn you." If he had said that, what hope for us could there be? Our problem is precisely that we do sin. There could be no forgiveness if forgiveness was based upon our ceasing to sin. Instead of that, Jesus actually spoke in the reverse order. First, he granted forgiveness freely, without any conceivable link to our performance. Forgiveness is granted only on the merit of his atoning death. But then, having forgiven us freely, Jesus tells us with equal force to stop sinning.

And here is the greatest wonder. There is nothing that can so motivate us as God's forgiveness.

Did the woman do it? I am sure she did. She had experienced grace in Jesus Christ, and that has always proved to be the most transforming life experience in the universe.

Have you learned that "grace and truth" came with Jesus Christ? Not all people have. I suppose it is fair to say that you are at some point in this story, whether you are aware of it or not. You may be in the position of the rulers, not necessarily in using your knowledge of what is right and wrong to come down hard on other people, though you may, but in merely going away when you are confronted by your need for forgiveness. The men in the story needed forgiveness as much as the woman. That is the meaning of their guilty withdrawal. But they did not find it since they left instead.

Or you may be like the crowd. The people were watching. They were spectators. They saw rulers' conviction and Jesus' compassion. They may even have marveled at both. But they did not enter into the action. Like many today, they stood at a distance and did not get involved.

Fortunately, there was also the woman. You may be like her. I hope you are. Of all the people who were present that day by far the best one to have been was the woman. For she not only witnessed the events. She experienced them, and that meant that she entered into the reality of Jesus' great grace.

The crowd did nothing except go home and forget what it had witnessed.

The rulers went from Jesus into increasing spiritual darkness, and six months later they were back again even more hardened than before to demand the death of the sinless Son of God. They had their law, but it did not save them. It hardened them, and they perished by it.

Only the sinful woman was saved, and it was because she had discovered that, although law had come through Moses and condemned her, grace and truth truly had come through Jesus Christ.

—from *The Glory of God's Grace*

The Grace of Wonder

BRENNAN MANNING

Several years before his death, a remarkable rabbi, Abraham Joshua Heschel, suffered a near-fatal heart attack. His closest male friend was at his bedside. Heschel was so weak he was only able to whisper: "Sam, I feel only gratitude for my life, for every moment I have lived. I am ready to go. I have seen so many miracles in my lifetime." The old rabbi was exhausted by his effort to speak. After a long pause, he said, "Sam, never once in my life did I ask God for success or wisdom or power or fame. I asked for wonder, and he gave it to me."

I asked for wonder, and he gave it to me. A Philistine will stand before a Claude Monet painting and pick his nose; a person filled with wonder will stand there fighting back the tears.

By and large, our world has lost its sense of wonder. We have grown up. We no longer catch our breath at the sight of a rainbow or the scent of a rose, as we once did. We have grown bigger and everything else smaller, less impressive. We get blasé and worldly wise and sophisticated. We no longer run our fingers through water, no longer shout at the stars or make faces at the moon. Water is H_2O, the stars have been classified, and the moon is not made of green cheese. Thanks to satellite TV and jet planes, we can visit places available in the past only to a Columbus, a Balboa, and other daring explorers.

There was a time in the not too distant past when a thunderstorm caused grown men to shudder and feel small. But God is being edged out of his world by science. The more we know about meteorology, the less inclined we are to pray during a thunderstorm. Airplanes now fly above, below, and around them. Satellites reduce them to photographs. What ignominy—if a thunderstorm could experience ignominy! Reduced from theophany to nuisance!

Heschel says that today we believe all enigmas can be solved, and all wonder is nothing but "the effect of novelty upon ignorance." Certainly, the new can amaze us: a space shuttle, the latest computer game, the softest diaper. Till tomorrow, till the new becomes old, till yesterday's wonder is discarded or taken for granted. Small wonder Rabbi Heschel concluded, "As civilization advances, the sense of wonder declines." . . .

Our world is saturated with grace, and the lurking presence of God is revealed not only in spirit but in matter—in a deer leaping across a meadow, in the flight of an eagle, in fire and water, in a rainbow after a summer storm, in a gentle doe streaking through a forest, in Beethoven's Ninth Symphony, in a child licking a chocolate ice cream cone, in a woman with windblown hair. God intended for us to discover His loving presence in the world around us. . . .

Living by the gospel of grace leads us into what Teilhard de Chardin called, "the divine milieu"—a God-filled, Christ-soaked universe, a world charged with the grandeur of God. How do we live in the presence of the living God? In wonder, amazed by the traces of God all around us.

Grace abounds in contemporary movies, books, novels, films, and music. If God is not in the whirlwind, He may be in a Woody Allen film or a Bruce Springsteen concert. Most people understand imagery and symbol better than doctrine and dogma. Images touch hearts and awaken imaginations. . . .

Will we ever understand the gospel of grace, the furious love of God, the world of grace in which we live? Jesus Christ is the scandal of God. When the Baptizer is imprisoned by Herod, he sends a couple of his followers to ask Jesus: "Are you the One who is to come into the world or should we wait for another?" Jesus says, "Go back and tell John what you have seen and heard: the blind see, the deaf hear, the lame walk, the poor have the gospel preached to them, the messianic era has erupted into history, and the love of my Father is revealed. Blessed is he who is not *scandalized* in me."

We should be astonished at the goodness of God, stunned that He should bother to call us by name, our mouths wide open at His love, bewildered that at this very moment we are standing on holy ground.

Every parable of mercy in the Bible was addressed by Jesus to His opponents: murmuring scribes, grumbling Pharisees, critical theologians, members of the Sanhedrin. They are the enemies of the gospel of grace, indignant because Jesus asserts that God cares about sinners, incensed that He should eat with people they despised. What does He tell them?

These sinners, these people you despise are nearer to God than you. It is not the hookers and thieves who find it most difficult to repent: it is you who are so secure in your piety and pretense that you have no need of conversion. They may have disobeyed God's call, their professions have debased them, but they have shown sorrow and repentance. But more than any of that, these are the people who appreciate His goodness: they are parading into the kingdom before you: for they have what you lack—a deep gratitude for God's love and deep wonder at His mercy.

Let us ask God for the gift He gave to an unforgettable rabbi, Joshua Abraham Heschel: "Dear Lord, grant me the grace of wonder. Surprise me, amaze me, awe me in every crevice of Your universe. Delight me to see how Your Christ plays in ten thousand places, lovely in limbs, and lovely in eyes not His, to the Father through the features of men's faces. Each day enrapture me with Your marvelous things without number. I do not ask to see the reason for it all; I ask only to share the wonder of it all."

—from *The Ragamuffin Gospel*

Manifold Grace

AMY CARMICHAEL

First Peter 1:6 and 4:10: *Manifold temptations: Manifold grace.*

The word "manifold" can be translated "many-colored." For every temptation there is grace. . . . God knows our many-colored temptations. He has many-colored grace to meet them—a color of grace for each temptation of evil. Will you try this plan? Pray instantly for the opposite grace to the temptation that attacks you. . . .

What is your temptation today? To despondency? cowardice? unlove? impatience? self-love? Temptations can be manifold. But pouring upon our souls is the sunlight of the grace of God, the many-folded, many-colored grace; we can take the grace we need: peacefulness that is happiness, courage that is victory, love that never loses hope, patience that is long-suffering with joyfulness, discipline—that which says "No" to self. There is something beyond our understanding in the way our wonderful God makes it possible for us to be that which naturally we are not. But let us leave all that, and in simple faith take His many-colored grace, "grace to help in time of need," "according to the measure of the gift of Christ," and that is immeasurable.

—from *Edges of His Ways*

All of Grace

Os Guinness

"What do you have that you did not receive?" Many of the greatest Christians of the centuries, including St. Augustine and St. Francis, have been influenced decisively by meditating on Paul's question to the church in Corinth. It admits only one answer: Nothing, for everything of God and good in our lives without a single exception is all of grace. That covers calling too. There is nothing fatalistic or arbitrary here. The motive, the initiative, and the action of calling are entirely God's and all of grace. Christ does not choose us because we are worth choosing, but simply because in his grace he loves us and chooses us—he calls us, in fact, despite all that he had to do to seal that choice in blood.

Without a due sense of gratitude, the "chosen people" would be insufferable. As Moses reminded the Jewish people, "The Lord did not set his affection on you and choose you because you were more numerous than other peoples, for you were the fewest of all peoples. But it was because the Lord loved you." Similarly King David was overwhelmed by the same wonder at his own calling as an individual, "Who am I, Lord God, and what is my family, that you have brought me this far? . . . There is no one like you, O Lord, and there is no God but you."

The grace that constitutes the cross also constitutes calling. Seen one way, calling initiates in our lives what the cross completes. Seen another, what the cross concludes beyond question as its final verdict, calling declares as its opening statement. Here is one relationship whose secret does not lie with us; self-conceit is absurd because our call to God is all of God and all of grace. Hilaire Belloc's famous short poem about the Jews applies to all who have been called:

> How odd
> of God
> to choose
> the Jews.

The link between calling and gratitude, chosenness and wonder touches our lives practically in two main places. First, it reminds us that with so much grace given to us, we should be givers of grace to others. Indeed, Jesus warns us in the parable of the unforgiving debtor, not to give grace to others after God has been so gracious to us is literally to double-deal God—and God will not stand for it. . . .

Second, the link between calling and grace reminds us that gratitude must be our first and constant response to God. The great Czech composer Anton'n Dvorak began writing his new music with the words, "with God" and ended "God be thanked." Similarly Johann Sebastian Bach wrote in the margins of his music "SDG" (*Soli Deo Gloria*) and "Glory to the Lamb."

Augustine described the Christian as an "alleluia from head to foot." George Herbert, a seventeenth-century Anglican poet, wrote a prayer in one of his poems, "You have given so much to me. Give me one thing more—a grateful heart." G. K. Chesterton stated as "the chief idea of my life" the practice of "taking things with gratitude and not taking things for granted." He passionately agreed with the artist Dante Gabriel Rossetti, "The worst moment for an atheist is when he is genuinely thankful, but has nobody to thank." And Chesterton remarked, typically, "If my children wake up on Christmas morning and have somebody to thank for putting candy into their stocking, have I no one to thank for putting two feet in mine?" W. H. Auden wrote simply, "Let your last thinks be all thanks."

Dostoevsky was so aware of the deep importance of gratitude in his own life that he was troubled for humankind if God were not there to be thanked: "Who is man going to love then?" he asks in *The Brothers Karamazov.* "To whom will he be thankful? To whom will he sing his hymn?" Only an idiot, he believed, could love and be grateful to humanity instead of God.

But whatever false turns secular culture may take, followers of Christ should know where they stand on this point—amazed and humbled ever to be chosen and called. Adapting G. K. Chesterton, we may state the motto of every follower of Christ moved to wonder by the mystery and grace of God's calling: "Nothing taken for granted; everything received with gratitude; everything passed on with grace."

—from *The Call*

Appreciating God's Grace

THOMAS À KEMPIS

Why do you look for rest when you were born to work? Resign yourself to patience rather than to comfort, to carrying your cross rather than to enjoyment. What man in the world, if he could always have them, would not readily accept consolation and spiritual joy, benefits which excel all earthly delights and pleasures of the body? The latter, indeed, are either vain or base, while spiritual joys, born of virtue and infused by God into pure minds, are alone truly pleasant and noble. Now, since the moment of temptation is always nigh, since false freedom of mind and overconfidence in self are serious obstacles to these visitations from heaven, a man can never enjoy them just as he wishes. God does well in giving the grace of consolation, but man does evil in not returning everything gratefully to God. Thus, the gifts of grace cannot flow in us when we are ungrateful to the Giver, when we do not return them to the Fountainhead. Grace is always given to him who is duly grateful, and what is wont to be given the humble will be taken away from the proud. I do not desire consolation that robs me of contrition, nor do I care for contemplation that leads to pride, for not all that is high is holy, nor is all that is sweet good, nor every desire pure, nor all that is dear to us pleasing to God. I accept willingly the grace whereby I become more humble and contrite, more willing to renounce self. The man who has been taught by the gift of grace, and who learns by the lash of its withdrawal, will never dare to attribute any good to himself, but will rather admit his poverty and emptiness. Give to God what is God's and ascribe to yourself what is yours. Give Him thanks, then, for His grace, but place upon yourself alone the blame and the punishment your fault deserves. Always take the lowest place and the highest will be given you, for the highest cannot exist apart from the lowest. The saints who are greatest before God are those who consider themselves the least, and the more humble they are within themselves, so much the more glorious they are. Since they do not desire vainglory, they are full of truth and heavenly glory. Being established and strengthened in God, they can by no means be proud. They attribute to God whatever good they have received; they seek no glory from one another but only that which comes from God alone. They desire above all things that He be praised in themselves and in all His saints—this is their constant purpose. Be grateful, therefore, for the least gift and you will be worthy to receive a greater. Consider the least gift as the greatest, the most contemptible as something special. And, if you but look to the dignity of the Giver, no gift will appear too small or worthless. Even though He give punishments and scourges, accept them, because He acts for our welfare in whatever He allows to befall us. He who desires to keep the grace of God ought to be grateful when it is given and patient when it is withdrawn. Let him pray that it return; let him be cautious and humble lest he lose it.

—from *The Imitation of Christ*

Effective Grace

EPHESIANS 3:1–12

For this reason I, Paul, the prisoner of Christ Jesus for you Gentiles—if indeed you have heard of the dispensation of the grace of God which was given to me for you, how that by revelation He made known to me the mystery (as I have briefly written already, by which, when you read, you may understand my knowledge in the mystery of Christ), which in other ages was not made known to the sons of men, as it has now been revealed by the Spirit to His holy apostles and prophets: that the Gentiles should be fellow heirs, of the same body, and partakers of His promise in Christ through the gospel, of which I became a minister according to the gift of the grace of God given to me by the effective working of His power.

To me, who am less than the least of all the saints, this grace was given, that I should preach among the Gentiles the unsearchable riches of Christ, and to make all see what is the fellowship of the mystery, which from the beginning of the ages has been hidden in God who created all things through Jesus Christ; to the intent that now the manifold wisdom of God might be made known by the church to the principalities and powers in the heavenly places, according to the eternal purpose which He accomplished in Christ Jesus our Lord, in whom we have boldness and access with confidence through faith in Him.

The Covenant of Grace

ANDREW MURRAY

The word *grace* is used in two senses. It is first the gracious disposition in God which moves Him to love us freely without our merit, and to bestow all His blessings upon us. Then it also means that power through which this grace does its work in us. The redeeming work of Christ, and the righteousness He won for us, equally with the work of the Spirit in us, as the power of the new life, are spoken of as Grace. It includes all that Christ has done and still does, all He has and gives, all He is for us and in us. John says, "We beheld His glory, the glory of the Only Begotten of the Father, full of grace and truth." "The law was given by Moses, grace and truth came by Jesus Christ." "And of His fullness have all we received, and grace for grace." What the law demands, grace supplies.

This contrast which John pointed out is expounded by Paul: "The law came in, that the offence might abound," and the way be prepared for the abounding of grace more exceedingly. The law points the way, but gives no strength to walk in it. The law demands, but makes no provision for its demands being met. The law burdens and condemns and slays. It can waken desire, but not satisfy it. It can rouse to effort, but not secure success. It can appeal to motives, but gives no inward power beyond what man himself has. And so, while warring against sin, it became its very ally in giving the sinner over to a hopeless condemnation. "The strength of sin is the law."

To deliver us from the bondage and the dominion of sin, grace came by Jesus Christ. Its work is twofold. Its exceeding abundance is seen in the free and full pardon there is of all transgression, in the bestowal of a perfect righteousness, and in the acceptance into God's favor and friendship. "In Him we have redemption through His blood, the forgiveness of sin according to the riches of His grace." It is not only at conversion and our admittance into God's favor, but throughout all our life, at each step of our way, and amid the highest attainments of the most advanced saint; we owe everything to grace, and grace alone. The thought of merit and work and worthiness is forever excluded.

The exceeding abundance of grace is equally seen in the work which the Holy Spirit every moment maintains within us. We have found that the central blessing of the New Covenant, flowing from Christ's redemption and the pardon of our sins, is the new heart in which God's law and fear and love have been put. It is in the fulfillment of this promise, in the maintenance of the heart in a state of meekness for God's indwelling, that the glory of grace is specially seen. In the very nature of things this must be so. Paul writes: "Where sin abounded, grace did more exceedingly abound." And where, as far as I was concerned, did sin abound? All the sin in earth and hell could not harm me, were it not for its presence in my heart. It is there it has exercised its terrible dominion. And it is there the exceeding abundance of grace must be proved, if it is to benefit me. All grace in earth and heaven could not help me; it is only in the heart it can be received, and known, and enjoyed. "Where sin abounded," in the heart, there "grace did more exceedingly abound; that as sin reigned in death," working its destruction in the heart and life, "even so might grace reign," in the heart too, "through righteousness into eternal life, through Jesus Christ our Lord." As had been said just before, "They that receive the abundance of grace shall reign in life through Jesus Christ."

Of this reign of grace in the heart Scripture speaks wondrous things. Paul speaks of the grace that fitted him for his work, of "the gift of that grace of God which was given me according to the working of His power." "The grace of our Lord was exceeding abundant, with faith and love." "The grace which was bestowed upon me was not found vain, but I laboured more abundantly than they all; yet not I, but the grace of God which was with me." "He said unto me, My grace is sufficient for thee; My strength is made perfect in weakness." He speaks in the same way of grace as working in the life of believers, when he exhorts them to "be strong in the grace that is in Christ Jesus"; when he tells us of "the grace of God" exhibited in the liberality of the Macedonian Christian, and "the exceeding grace of God" in the Corinthians; when he encourages them: "God is able to make all grace abound in you, that ye may abound unto every good work." Grace is not only the power that moves the heart of God in its compassion towards us, when He acquits and accepts the sinner and makes him a child, but is equally the power that moves the heart of the saint, and provides it each moment with just the disposition and the power which it needs to love God and do His will.

It is impossible to speak too strongly of the need there is to know that, as wonderful and free and alone sufficient as is the grace that pardons, is the grace that sanctifies; we are just as absolutely dependent upon the latter as the former. We can do as little to the one as the other. The grace that works in us must as exclusively do all in us and through us as the grace that pardons does all for us. In the one case as the other, everything is by faith alone. Not to apprehend this brings a double danger. On the one hand, people think that grace cannot be more exalted than in the bestowal of pardon on the vile and unworthy; and a secret feeling arises that, if God be so magnified by our sins more than anything else, we must not expect to be freed from them in this life. With many this cuts at the root of the life of true holiness. On the other hand, from not knowing that grace is always and alone to do all the work in our sanctification and fruitbearing, men are thrown upon their own efforts, their life remains one of feebleness and bondage under the law, and they never yield themselves to let grace do all it would.

Let us listen to what God's Word says: "By grace have ye been saved, through faith; not of works, lest any man should glory. For we are His workmanship, created in Christ Jesus for good works, which God afore prepared that we should walk in them." Grace stands in contrast to good works of our own not only before conversion, but after conversion too. We are created in Christ Jesus for good works, which God had prepared for us. It is grace alone can work them in us and work them out through us. Not only the commencement but the continuance of the Christian life is the work of grace. "Now if it is by grace it is no more of works, otherwise grace is no more grace; therefore it is of faith that it may be according to grace." As we see that grace is literally and absolutely to do all in us, so that all our actings are the showing forth of grace in us, we shall consent to live the life of faith, a life in which, every moment, everything is expected from God. It is only then that we shall experience that sin shall not, never, not for a moment, have dominion over us.

"Ye are not under the law, but under grace." There are three possible lives. One entirely under the law; one entirely under grace; one a mixed life, partly law, partly grace. It is this last against which Paul warns the Romans. It is this which is so common, and works such ruin among Christians. Let us find out whether this is not our position, and the cause of our low state. Let us beseech God to open our eyes by the Holy Spirit to see that in the New Covenant everything, every movement, every moment of our Christian life, is of grace, abounding grace; grace abounding exceedingly, and working mightily. Let us believe that our Covenant God waits to cause all grace to abound toward us. And let us begin to live the life of faith that depends upon, and trusts in, and looks to, and ever waits for God, through Jesus Christ, by the Holy Spirit, to work in us that which is pleasing in His sight.

Grace unto you, and peace be multiplied!

—from *Two Covenants*

Blessed Assurance

MARTIN LUTHER

This inner assurance of the grace of God is accompanied by outward indications such as gladly to hear, preach, praise, and to confess Christ, to do one's duty in the station in which God has placed us, to aid the needy, and to comfort the sorrowing. These are the affidavits of the Holy Spirit testifying to our favorable standing with God.

If we could be fully persuaded that we are in the good grace of God, that our sins are forgiven, that we have the Spirit of Christ, that we are the beloved children of God, we would be ever so happy and grateful to God. But because we often feel fear and doubt we cannot come to that happy certainty.

Train your conscience to believe that God approves of you. Fight it out with doubt. Gain assurance through the Word of God.

—from *Commentary on Galatians*

Grace for Service

Dwight L. Moody

I heard a story about two members of a church: one was a wealthy man, and the other was one of those who cannot take care of their finances—he was always in debt. The rich brother had compassion on his poor brother. He wanted to give him some money; but he would not give it to the man all at once: he knew he would not use it properly. So he sent the amount to the minister, and asked him to supply the needs of this poor brother. The minister used to send him a five-dollar bill, and put on the envelope "More to follow." I can imagine how welcome the gift would be; but the best of all was the promise—"More to follow." So it is with God: there is always "more to follow." It is such a pity that we are not ready to be used by God when He wants to use us.

Dear friends, let me put this question to you: Are you full of grace? You shake your head. Well, it is our privilege to be *full*. What is the best way to get full of grace? It is to be emptied of self. How can we be emptied? Suppose you wish to get the air out of this tumbler; how can you do it? I will tell you: by pouring water into the tumbler till it is full to overflowing. That is the way the Lord empties us of self. He fills us with His grace. "I will pour water on him that is thirsty." Are you hungering to get rid of your sinful selves? Then let the Spirit of God come in and fill you. God is able to do it.

See what He did for John Bunyan—how He made one of the mightiest instruments for good the world ever saw, out of that swearing Bedford tinker. If we had a telescope which would enable us to look into heaven as Stephen did, I can imagine we should see the thief, who believed in Jesus while on the cross, very near the throne. Ask him how he got there, and he would tell you it was through the grace of God. See how the grace of God could save a Mary Magdalene possessed of seven devils! Ask her what it was that melted her heart, and she would tell you that it was the grace of God. Look again at that woman whom Christ met at the well at Sychar. The Saviour offered her a cup of the living water: she drank, and now she walks the crystal pavement of heaven. See how the grace of God could change Zaccheus, the hated publican of Jericho! Now he is in yonder world of light; he was brought there by the sovereign grace of God.

You will have noticed that many of those who were about the most unlikely, have, by the power of God's grace, become very eminent in His service. Look at the twelve apostles of Christ; they were all unlettered men. This ought to encourage all whose education is limited to give themselves to God's work. When our earthly work is ended, then, like our Master, we shall enter into glory. It has been well remarked: "Grace is glory militant; and glory is grace triumphant. Grace is glory begun; glory is grace made perfect. Grace is the first degree of glory: glory is the highest degree of grace."

—from *Sovereign Grace*

Galilean Grace

Peter's life was never again the same after that catch.

He had turned his back on the sea to follow the Messiah. He had left the boats thinking he'd never return. But now he's back. Full circle. Same sea. Same boat. Maybe even the same spot.

But this isn't the same Peter. Three years of living with the Messiah have changed him. He's seen too much. Too many walking crippled, vacated graves, too many hours hearing his words. He's not the same Peter. It's the same Galilee, but a different fisherman.

Why did he return? What brought him back to Galilee after the crucifixion? Despair? Some think so—I don't. Hope dies hard for a man who has known Jesus. I think that's what Peter has. That's what brought him back. Hope. A bizarre hope that on the sea where he knew him first, he would know him again.

So Peter is in the boat, on the lake. Once again he's fished all night. Once again the sea has surrendered nothing.

His thoughts are interrupted by a shout from the shore. "Catch any fish?" Peter and John look up. Probably a villager. "No!" they yell. "Try the other side!" the voice yells back. John looks at Peter. What harm? So out sails the net. Peter wraps the rope around his wrist to wait.

But there is no wait. The rope pulls taut and the net catches. Peter sets his weight against the side of the boat and begins to bring in the net; reaching down, pulling up, reaching down, pulling up. He's so intense with the task, he misses the message.

John doesn't. The moment is déjà vu. This has happened before. The long night. The empty net. The call to cast again. Fish flapping on the floor of the boat. Wait a minute. He lifts his eyes to the man on the shore. "It's him," he whispers.

Then louder, "It's Jesus."

Then shouting, "It's the Lord, Peter. It's the Lord!"

Peter turns and looks. Jesus has come. Not just Jesus the teacher, but Jesus the death-defeater, Jesus the king . . . Jesus the victor over darkness. Jesus the God of heaven and earth is on the shore . . . and he's building a fire.

Peter plunges into the water, swims to the shore, and stumbles out wet and shivering and stands in front of the friend he betrayed. Jesus has prepared a bed of coals. Both are aware of the last time Peter had stood near a fire. Peter had failed God, but God had come to him.

For one of the few times in his life, Peter is silent. What words would suffice? The moment is too holy for words. God is offering breakfast to the friend who betrayed him. And Peter is once again finding grace at Galilee.

—from *He Still Moves Stones*

A Drop of Grace

JOHN TAULER

All works which men and all creatures can ever work even to the end of the world, without the grace of God—all of them together, however great they may be, are an absolute nothing, as compared with the smallest work which God has worked in men by His grace. As much as God is better than all His creatures, so much better are His works than all the works, or wisdom, or designs, which all men could devise. Even the smallest drop of grace is better than all earthly riches that are beneath the sun. Yea, a drop of grace is more noble than all angels and all souls, and all the natural things that God has made. And yet grace is given more richly by God to the soul than any earthly gift. It is given more richly than brooks of water, than the breath of the air, than the brightness of the sun; for spiritual things are far finer and nobler than earthly things. The whole Trinity, Father, Son, and Holy Ghost, give grace to the soul, and flow immediately into it; even the highest angel, in spite of his great nobility, cannot do this. Grace looses us from the snares of many temptations; it relieves us from the heavy burden of worldly cares, and carries the spirit up to heaven, the land of spirits. It kills the worm of conscience, which makes sins alive. Grace is a very powerful thing. The man, to whom cometh but a little drop of the light of grace, to him all that is not God becomes as bitter as gall upon the tongue.

Grace makes, contrary to nature, all sorrows sweet, and brings it about that a man no longer feels any relish for things which formerly gave him great pleasure and delight. On the other hand, what formerly disgusted him, now delights him and is the desire of his heart—for instance, weakness, sorrow, inwardness, humility, self-abandonment, and detachment from all the creatures. All this is in the highest degree dear to him, when this visitation of the Holy Ghost, grace, has in truth come to him. Then the sick man, that is to say the external man, with all his faculties is plunged completely into the pool of water, even as the sick man who had been for thirty-eight years by the pool at Jerusalem, and there washes himself thoroughly in the exalted, noble, precious blood of Christ Jesus. For grace in manifold ways bathes the soul in the wounds and blood of the holy Lamb, Jesus Christ.

—from *Light, Life, and Love*

A Holy Sonnet

JOHN DONNE

At the earth's round imagined corners, blow
Your trumpets, angels; and arise, arise
From death, you numberless infinities
Of souls, and to your scattered bodies go:
All whom the flood did, and fire shall, o'erthrow,
All whom war, dearth, age, agues, tyrannies,
Despair, law, chance hath slain, and you whose eyes
Shall behold God, and never taste death's woe.
But let them sleep, Lord, and me mourn a space;
For, if above all these, my sins abound,
'Tis late to ask abundance of Thy grace
When we are there. Here on this lowly ground,
Teach me how to repent; for that's as good
As if Thou hadst sealed my pardon with Thy blood.

Further Up and Further In

C. S. LEWIS

"Kings and Queens," he cried, "we have all been blind. We are only beginning to see where we are. From up there I have seen it all— Ettinsmuir, Beaversdam, the Great River, and Cair Paravel still shining on the edge of the Eastern Sea. Narnia is not dead. This is Narnia."

"But how can it be?" said Peter. "For Aslan told us older ones that we should never return to Narnia, and here we are."

"Yes," said Eustace. "And we saw it all destroyed and the sun put out."

"And it's all so different," said Lucy.

"The Eagle is right," said the Lord Digory. "Listen, Peter. When Aslan said you could never go back to Narnia, he meant the Narnia you were thinking of. But that was not the real Narnia. That had a beginning and an end. It was only a shadow or a copy of the real Narnia which has always been here and always will be here: just as our own world, England and all, is only a shadow or copy of something in Aslan's real world. You need not mourn over Narnia, Lucy. All of the old Narnia that mattered, all the dear creatures, have been drawn into the real Narnia through the Door. And of course it is different; as different as a real thing is from a shadow or as waking life is from a dream." . . .

It is as hard to explain how this sunlit land was different from the old Narnia as it would be to tell you how the fruits of that country taste. Perhaps you will get some idea of it if you think like this.

You may have been in a room in which there was a window that looked out on a lovely bay of the sea or a green valley that wound away among the mountains. And in the wall of that room opposite to the window there may have been a looking-glass. And as you turned away from the window you suddenly caught sight of that sea or that valley, all over again, in the looking-glass. And the sea in the mirror, or the valley in the mirror, were in one sense just the same as the real ones: yet at the same time they were somehow different—deeper, more wonderful, more like places in a story: in a story you have never heard but very much want to know. The difference between the old Narnia and the new Narnia was like that. The new one was a deeper country: every rock and flower and blade of grass looked as if it meant more. I can't describe it any better than that: if you ever get there you will know what I mean.

It was the Unicorn who summed up what everyone was feeling. He stamped his right forehoof on the ground and neighed, and then cried:

"I have come home at last! This is my real country! I belong here. This is the land I have been looking for all my life, though I never knew it till now. The reason why we loved the old Narnia is that it sometimes looked a little like this. Bree-hee-hee! Come further up, come further in!"

—from *The Last Battle*

The Reign of Grace

SCOTTY SMITH

God's grace is given freely and undeservedly, but not without intent and implications. We dare not try to privatize or domesticate the significance of God's grace. We have been called into a dynamic love affair—one that gives more than we would freely give. To receive God's grace in Christ is to be brought into a revolutionary reign, not ushered into a quiet rest home! God's love is as disruptive as it is delightful, as demanding as it is delicious! God loves us exactly as we are today, but he loves us too much to leave us as we are and where we are.

Grace is free, but not frail! The Scriptures attest over and over to the potent and life-giving effect that grace is to have in our lives as it reigns supreme in our hearts.

- We are to "grow in the grace and knowledge of our Lord and Savior, Jesus Christ." (2 Pet. 3:18)

- We must be careful not to "receive God's grace in vain" (2 Cor. 6:1) by having disregard for Jesus, his cross, and his kingdom.

- We must not "set aside the grace of God" (Gal. 2:21) by reverting to self-righteousness.

- The grace of God is not to be "without effect" (1 Cor. 15:10) in our lives, a mere cosmetic window treatment.

- To revert to salvation by obedience is to have "fallen away from grace." (Gal. 5:4)

- We are to submit to the pedagogy of grace, for it "teaches us to say 'No' to ungodliness and worldly passions, and to live self-controlled, upright and godly lives in this present age." (Titus 2:12 NIV)

- Grace does not eliminate or leapfrog us over our weaknesses and limitations; on the contrary, "grace is sufficient" to bring God's power into the very things we despise, like insults, hardships, persecutions, and difficulties. (2 Cor. 12:8–10)

- Grace doesn't make us guiltless couch potatoes in the kingdom, rather, "to each one of us grace has been given" so we can do our part to "fill the whole universe" with the glory of Jesus. (Eph. 4:7–16)

- When we choose to live disobedient lives—indifferent to the glory of God, we aren't insulated by grace, we insult "the Spirit of grace." (Heb. 10:28–31)

- Indeed, God hasn't lavished grace upon us to release us from concerns about holiness but so that "grace might reign through righteousness." (Rom. 5:20–21)

If grace is to have its transforming way in our lives, we must submit to it as loyal, devoted servants submit unquestionably to a king. We who have been made objects of God's tender affection have also been made subjects in his transforming kingdom, servants of the era of "new creation," participants in the reign of grace.

—from *The Reign of Grace*

INSTRUMENTS

OF

GRACE

*And God is able to make all grace abound toward you,
that you, always having all sufficiency in all things,
may have an abundance for every good work.*

— 2 CORINTHIANS 9:8

I would far rather convey grace than explain it.

— PHILIP YANCEY

Beggars in Need of Bread

MAX LUCADO

We are sinners in need of grace, strugglers in need of strength. Jesus teaches us to pray, "Forgive our debts . . . and lead us not into temptation."

We've all made mistakes and we'll all make some more. The line that separates the best of us from the worst of us is a narrow one, hence we'd be wise to take seriously Paul's admonition: *Why do you judge your brothers or sisters in Christ? And why do you think you are better than they? We will all stand before the Lord to be judged. . . .* (Rom. 14:10).

Your sister would like me to remind you that she needs grace. Just like you need forgiveness, so does she. There comes a time in every relationship when it's damaging to seek justice, when settling the score only stirs the fire. There comes a time when the best thing you can do is accept your brother and offer him the same grace you've been given.

—from *The Great House of God*

Five Polluted Words

PHILIP YANCEY

One day my wife, Janet, who was directing a senior citizens' program in one of Chicago's poorest neighborhoods, came across this quote: "The poor express their gratitude not by saying thanks but by asking for more." She had just spent an exhausting day, and felt besieged by whiny, insistent demands for ever more help. The quote proved strangely comforting, she told me.

Why is it that the poor express their gratitude so indirectly? I wondered. Why don't they simply give thanks? After talking to Janet about her many experiences on the job, I concluded it is because of shame—shame over their need for help in the first place. I know how hard it is for me to ask someone else for help. What would it be like to live in a constant state of neediness?

More to the point, how can those of us who give to others do so without somehow undermining their sense of dignity? Due to my writer's instinct, I immediately started thinking of individual words, and I began to make a list of these words. All of them began as a pure expression of *giving* but became polluted over time. Such words litter the English language; taken together, they offer a strong warning about the dangers inherent in giving and receiving.

Pity. Deriving from the same root as *piety* and *pious,* this word once denoted a high form of sacrificial love. God, a perfect being without needs, nevertheless chose to give of himself to his creatures. God had pity on needy people, such as the Israelite slaves in Egypt.

God's ultimate act of self-giving, the Incarnation, can actually be seen as an act of pity, motivated out of God's love for us fallen human creatures. On earth, Jesus often felt moved with compassion, or pity. Those who mimicked him—the rich having "pity" on the poor, for example—thus expressed Godlike qualities.

That was the older meaning of the word, at least. Eventually, emphasis shifted from the givers of pity to the recipients, who were seen as weak and inferior. Now we hear the taunt, "I don't want your pity!" One who shows pity is condescending, even *un*loving—the meaning of the word has clearly inverted.

Charity. The IRS still recognizes the inherent goodness of the word—the agency grants tax exemptions to "charitable" organizations—but surely it, too, has lost some luster. In the Bible's King James Version of 1611, 1 Corinthians 13 renders *charity* as a direct translation of *agape*, the most exalted form of love. Charity flows from a person who is patient, kind, forgiving, humble; charity never fails to discern the best in people.

Yet once again the meaning inverted over time: now no one wants to be a charity case. We accept charity only in desperation, as a last resort.

Condescend. I view the Bible as a step-by-step history of God's condescensions. To Adam in the garden, to Moses in the burning bush, to the Israelites in the glory cloud, and finally to all of us in the Incarnation, he con- (meaning *with*) descended, or "descended to be with" us.

A true Christian follows that example, as the apostle Paul clearly outlined in this passage: "Your attitude should be the same as that of Christ Jesus: Who, being in very nature God, did not consider equality with God something to be grasped, but made himself nothing, taking the very nature of a servant, being made in human likeness" (Philippians 2:5–7 NIV).

Once again, though, over time the word's meaning leaked away. We have lost the fine art of condescension. Who of us would welcome the remark, "You're so condescending!"

Patronize. I have a special fondness for this word, for artists, musicians, and, yes, writers were once relieved of everyday anxieties about earning a living due to the generosity of *patrons.* Nowadays, however, there are few patrons, and fewer still who would want to be called patronizing. The *Random House Webster's Dictionary* defines *patronize* as "to behave in an offensively *condescending* manner toward"!

Paternalism. Another fine word, badly tainted. The root comes from *pater,* or "father." In older days, a paternalistic person reminded others of a kindly father who cared for the needs of his children; now the system more resembles an insensitive stepfather who reeks of superiority as he stoops down to help his charges.

Why have these words changed in meaning? Each of them, once honorable and majestic, gradually melted like a wax statue into a sad lump barely resembling its former self. The words have changed, quite simply, because we humans have failed so often and so badly at the difficult task of giving. Perhaps an ancient Chinese proverb expresses the problem best: "Nothing atones for the insult of a gift but the love of the giver."

A Christian organization carrying out relief work in a needy country, my wife as she ministers one-on-one to senior citizens or the homeless, I as I confront a beggar on the street—each of us confronts the vast and perilous gap between the giver and the receiver. Government programs established with the highest of motives often founder for reasons that can be glimpsed in these polluted words. An institution cannot love; only people can love. As the proverb says, apart from love, giving becomes an insult.

We could all avoid these problems if we simply ignored the needy and associated with self-sufficient people exclusively. However, reaching out to the needy is not an option for the Christian. It is a command. I wrote a book entitled *Where Is God When It Hurts?* The real answer to that question, the answer implicit in the New Testament, is another question: Where is the church when it hurts? We followers of Jesus are God's primary response to the massive needs of the world. We are literally Christ's body.

When Jesus lived here in a physical body, he spent time among the poor, the widowed, the paralyzed, and even those with dreaded diseases. People with leprosy, for example—the AIDS patients of ancient times—were required to cry out, "Unclean! Unclean!" if anyone approached; touching such a person went against the laws of Moses. Yet Jesus defied law and custom by going up to leprosy patients and touching them—an act of astonishing condescension. That has been God's consistent pattern in all of history.

We in the church, God's body on earth, are likewise called to move toward those who suffer. We are, after all, God's means of expressing his love to the world, which is why words such as *pity* and *charity* originated as religious words.

Can we reclaim these polluted words—or, if not the words,

then at least the meaning behind them? I take hope in the fact that all the words in the above list retain at least a glimmer of their theological origin. There is a way to make pity Godlike; charity can convey a high form of love; condescension may lead to unity, not division; a patron may exalt, not demean, his subjects; paternalism may, in fact, remind us of our true state as children of a heavenly Father.

Indeed, I only know of one way to eliminate the great gap between giver and receiver, and that is a humble recognition that all of us are needy beggars, sustained each moment by the mercy of a sovereign God. Only as we experience God's grace as pure grace, not something we earned or worked for, can we offer love with no strings attached to another person in need. There is but one true Giver in the universe; all else are debtors.

—from *Finding God in Unexpected Places*

A Prayer for Grace

JANE AUSTEN

Incline us, O God,

to think humbly of ourselves,

to be saved only in the examination of our own conduct,

to consider our fellow-creatures with kindness,

and to judge of all they say and do with the charity

which we would desire from them ourselves.

The Law of Love

CYNTHIA HEALD

In a "Peanuts" episode by cartoonist Charles Schulz, Lucy declared to Linus, "I love mankind; it's people I can't stand." I readily understand Lucy's dilemma. I can be so committed to loving others when I am alone, but let me go out of my room and I am continually challenged to be kind and loving.

As I have tried to understand why it is hard for me to love others sincerely, I have come to realize the depth of my selfishness and strong commitment to protect my "rights." I have a right to be loved first; I have a right to be treated kindly; I have a right not to suffer; I have a right to repay those who hurt me. Why should I love those who are unkind? How can I love those who wound me? How can I be expected to lay down *my* life for those who don't appreciate me? Why should I be asked to love others, not just as I love myself, but as Christ loves me, unconditionally—no *ifs, ands,* or *buts?*

It is hard, but it is the law of Christ. And if I am His child and I want to please Him, I need to obey. But *why* is this the law of Christ? Why are we asked to fulfill this one command? One of the reasons we are asked to love in this way is that it is the very best way for us to live. Love is the excellent way. Love heals. Love blesses not only the recipient but also the giver. It frees the lover from having to protect self. Love is full of grace.

Anger and bitterness destroy and divide. Anger and bitterness demand retribution and require great emotional energy. They produce anxiety, tension, and loss of hope. God doesn't want us to live this way. *It is because He loves us that He has commanded us to love. We can love because we are loved perfectly by Him.* His love is enough. He is our protector and shield; we no longer have to defend ourselves or battle for our rights. He has promised to repay any wrongs we have suffered. We are free to experience the freedom and blessing of forgiveness. We can rest in His justice and mercy. We can now just love and be loved—because He is the God of all grace.

—from *Becoming a Woman of Grace*

The Temper

GEORGE HERBERT

How should I praise Thee, Lord! How should my rhymes
Gladly engrave Thy love in steel,
If what my soul doth feel sometimes,
My soul might ever feel!

Although there were some forty heav'ns, or more,
Sometimes I peer above them all;
Sometimes I hardly reach a score;
Sometimes to hell I fall.

O rack me not to such a vast extent;
Those distances belong to Thee:
The world's too little for Thy tent,
A grave too big for me.

Wilt Thou meet arms with man, that Thou dost stretch
A crumb of dust from heav'n to hell?
Will great God measure with a wretch?
Shall he Thy stature spell?

O let me, when Thy roof my soul hath hid,
O let me roost and nestle there:
Then of a sinner Thou art rid,
And I of hope and fear.

Yet take Thy way; for sure Thy way is best:
Stretch or contract me Thy poor debtor:
This is but tuning of my breast,
To make the music better.

Whether I fly with angels, fall with dust,
Thy hands made both, and I am there;
Thy power and love, my love and trust,
Make one place ev'rywhere.

Love Your Enemies

"You have heard that it was said, 'An eye for an eye and a tooth for a tooth.' But I tell you not to resist an evil person. But whoever slaps you on your right cheek, turn the other to him also. If anyone wants to sue you and take away your tunic, let him have your cloak also. And whoever compels you to go one mile, go with him two. Give to him who asks you, and from him who wants to borrow from you do not turn away.

"You have heard that it was said, 'You shall love your neighbor and hate your enemy.' But I say to you, love your enemies, bless those who curse you, do good to those who hate you, and pray for those who spitefully use you and persecute you, that you may be sons of your Father in heaven; for He makes His sun rise on the evil and on the good, and sends rain on the just and on the unjust. For if you love those who love you, what reward have you? Do not even the tax collectors do the same? And if you greet your brethren only, what do you do more than others? Do not even the tax collectors do so? Therefore you shall be perfect, just as your Father in heaven is perfect."

Responding to Grace

BRENNAN MANNING

We're graced and made beautiful by God's irreversible forgiveness, his endless patience, his tender love. We're healed and made whole by the gentle Spirit dwelling within us. We're empowered to live lives of joy and wonder captivated by the undeserved promise of the Kingdom. Everything we have and are as humans and Christians derives from divine goodness and kindness.

What response does the Father seek in return for his relentless tenderness? Personal experience has taught us that illusion and self-deception are no strangers to the spiritual life. What gives the ring of truth and the stamp of authenticity to the Christian's response to Abba's love, the firm assurance that she isn't deceiving herself?

The answer is neither vague nor ambiguous. Speaking first through the voice of his beloved Son, Abba says,

"Come, you have your Father's blessing! Inherit the Kingdom prepared for you from the creation of the world." Why do I declare you blessed and beneficiaries of the Kingdom? Because the only Son I've ever had was hungry and you gave him food, he was thirsty and you gave him a drink. He was a stranger and you welcomed him, naked and you clothed him. He was ill and you comforted him, in prison and you came to visit him. Then you just ones will ask me, "Abba, when did we see your beloved Son hungry and give him food or see him thirsty and give him a drink? When did we welcome him away from home or clothe him in his nakedness? When did we visit him when he was ill or in prison?" I will answer them: "I assure you, as often as you did it for one of your least brothers and sisters, you did it for my only-begotten Son." [Here I've taken the words of Jesus in Matt. 25:34–40 and have them originate from the Father. The essential meaning of the passage stays the same.]

To pray Abba in the Spirit is to make our interior life resemble that of Jesus and to become a son or daughter in the Son (*filii in Filio*). "The proof that you are sons is the fact that God has sent forth into our heart the spirit of his Son which cries out, 'Abba!' ('Father')" (Gal. 4:6). With the Spirit in our hearts, we have a living faith-experience; and living faith, according to Paul, "expresses itself in love" (Gal. 5:6).

Exaggeration and overstatement aren't the dangers here. Love is the axis of the Christian moral revolution and the only sign by which the disciple is to be recognized (John 13:35). The danger lurks in our subtle attempts to minimize, rationalize, or justify our moderation in this regard.

The response the Father seeks to his extravagant generosity, and the sign that we're living in the wisdom of tenderness, is that we love, honor, serve, and revere his only Son as he manifests himself in the least of the brethren. "The word you hear is not mine; it comes from the Father who sent me," Jesus tells us (John 14:24). The willingness to live for others is a more accurate measure of our love for Jesus than ecstasy in prayer. As Thomas Merton put it, "Without love and compassion for others, our own apparent love for Christ is a fiction."

When I live no longer for myself, I can be open to God and open to my neighbor, whom God accepts just as he accepts me. . . .

In the imagery of the parables, God is presented as the father rushing out to meet his son, the absurdly generous farmer who gives latecomers the same wage as day-long laborers, the judge hearing the prayer of the importunate widow. In the man Jesus, the invisible God becomes visible and audible. And he's seen as a God "whose tender compassion has broken from on high, to shine on those who dwell in darkness and the shadow of death, and to guide our feet on the road to peace" (Luke 1:78–79). The prophet Jesus taught in the power of the Spirit that Christian giving and forgiving should copy God's giving and forgiving. Acceptance is absolute—without inquiry into the past, without special conditions—so that the liberated sinner can live again, accept her self, forgive her self, love her self.

As Christians living in the Spirit, we're called to pass on the tenderness of God. The parameters of our compassion extend beyond those who opt for our lifestyle, favor our existence, or make us feel good. Charges of elitism are dropped for the lack of evidence. Peace and reconciliation for all, without exception—even for moral failures—is the radical lifestyle of Christians living in the wisdom of accepted tenderness. We may be called friends of tax-collectors and sinners—but only because we are (or should be). We understand that we're in the company of some rather honorable people, those sinners; in fact, we're in the company of Jesus himself. According to the gospel, it's unrestrained tenderness and limitless compassion that stamp our relationship with the Father of Jesus as belonging to the order of the Really Real.

—from *The Wisdom of Tenderness*

How the Great Guest Came

EDWIN MARKHAM

Before the cathedral in grandeur rose
At Ingelburg where the Danube goes;
Before its forest of silver spires
Went airily up to the clouds and fires;
Before the oak had ready a beam,
While yet the arch was stone and dream—
There, where the altar was later laid,
Conrad, the cobbler, plied his trade.

It happened one day at the year's white end—
Two neighbors called on their old-time friend;
And they found the shop, so meager and mean,
Made gay with a hundred boughs of green.
Conrad was stitching with face ashine,
But suddenly stopped as he twitched a twine:
"Old friends, good news! At dawn today,
As the cocks were scaring the night away,
The Lord appeared in a dream to me,
And said, 'I am coming—your Guest to be!'
So I've been busy with feet astir,
Strewing the floor with branches of fir.

The wall is washed and the shelf is shined,
And over the rafter the holly twined.
He comes today, and the table is spread
With milk and honey and wheaten bread."

His friends went home; and his face grew still
As he watched for the shadow across the sill.
He lived all the moments o'er and o'er,
When the Lord should enter his lowly door—
The knock, the call, the latch pulled up,
The lighted face, the offered cup.
He would wash the feet where the spikes had been,
He would kiss His hands where the nails went in,
And then at the last would sit with Him
And break the bread till the day grew dim.

While the cobbler mused there passed his pane
A beggar drenched by the driving rain.
He called him in from the stony street
And gave him shoes for his bruisèd feet.

The beggar went and there came a crone,
Her face with wrinkles of sorrow sown.
A bundle of fagots bowed her back,
And she was spent with the wrench and rack.
He gave her the loaf and steadied her load
As she took her way on the weary road.

Then to his door came a little child,
Lost and afraid in the world so wild,
In the big, dark world. Catching it up,
He gave it the milk in the waiting cup,
And led it home to its mother's arms,
Out of the reach of the world's alarms.

The day went down in the crimson west
And with it his hope of the blessed Guest,
And Conrad sighed as the world turned gray:
"Why is it, Lord, that your feet delay?
Did you forget that this was the day?"

Then, soft in the silence, a Voice he heard:
"Lift up your spirit, for I kept my word.
Three times I came to your friendly door;
Three times my shadow was on your floor.
I was the beggar with bruisèd feet;
I was the woman you gave to eat;
I was the child on the homeless street!"

The Divine Nature of Grace

THOMAS À KEMPIS

The Disciple: O Lord, my God, who created me to Your own image and likeness, grant me this grace which You have shown to be so great and necessary for salvation, that I may overcome my very evil nature that is drawing me to sin and perdition. For I feel in my flesh the law of sin contradicting the law of my mind and leading me captive to serve sensuality in many things. I cannot resist the passions thereof unless Your most holy grace warmly infused into my heart assist me.

There is need of Your grace, and of great grace, in order to overcome a nature prone to evil from youth. For through the first man, Adam, nature is fallen and weakened by sin, and the punishment of that stain has fallen upon all mankind. Thus nature itself, which You created good and right, is considered a symbol of vice and the weakness of corrupted nature, because when left to itself tends toward evil and to baser things. The little strength remaining in it is like a spark hidden in ashes. That strength is natural reason which, surrounded by thick darkness, still had the power of judging good and evil, of seeing the difference between true and false, though it is not able to fulfill all that it approves and does not enjoy the full light or soundness of affection.

Hence it is, my God, that according to the inward man I delight in Your law, knowing that Your command is good, just, and holy, and that it proved the necessity of shunning all evil and sin. But in the flesh I keep the law of sin, obeying sensuality rather than reason. Hence, also, it is that the will to good is present in me, but how to accomplish it I know not. Hence, too, I often propose many good things, but because the grace to help my weakness is lacking, I recoil and give up at the slightest resistance. Thus it is that I know the way of perfection and see clearly enough how I ought to act, but because I am pressed down by the weight of my own corruption I do not rise to more perfect things.

How extremely necessary to me, O Lord, Your grace is to begin any good deed, to carry it on and bring it to completion! For without grace I can do nothing, but with its strength I can do all things in You. O Grace truly heavenly, without which our merits are nothing, no gifts of nature are to be esteemed!

Before You, O Lord, not arts or riches, no beauty or strength, no wit or intelligence avail without grace. For the gifts of nature are common to good and bad alike, but the peculiar gift of Your elect is grace or love, and those who are signed with it are held worthy of everlasting life. So excellent is this grace that without it no gift of prophecy or of miracles, no meditation be it ever so exalted, can be considered anything. Not even faith or hope or other virtues are acceptable to You without charity and grace.

O most blessed grace, which makes the poor in spirit rich in virtues, which renders him who is rich in many things humble of heart, come, descend upon me, fill me quickly with your consolation lest my soul faint with weariness and dryness of mind.

Let me find grace in Your sight, I beg, Lord, for Your grace is enough for me, even though I obtain none of the things which nature desires. If I am tempted and afflicted with many tribulations, I will fear no evils while Your grace is with me. This is my strength. This will give me counsel and help. This is more powerful than all my enemies and wiser than all the wise. This is the mistress of truth, the teacher of discipline, the light of the heart, the consoler in anguish, the banisher of sorrow, the expeller of fear, the nourisher of devotion, the producer of tears. What am I without grace, but dead wood, a useless branch, fit only to be cast away?

Let Your grace, therefore, go before me and follow me, O Lord, and make me always intent upon good works, through Jesus Christ, Your Son.

—from *The Imitation of Christ*

Dispatch from the Culture Wars

PHILIP YANCEY

People in Jesus' time who looked to him as their political savior were constantly befuddled by his choice of companions. He became known as a friend of tax collectors, a group clearly identified with the foreign exploiters. Though he denounced the religious system of his day, he treated a leader like Nicodemus with respect, and though he spoke against the dangers of money and of violence, he showed love and compassion toward a rich young ruler and a Roman centurion.

In short, Jesus honored the dignity of each person whether he agreed with him or her or not. Anyone, even a half-breed with five husbands or a thief nailed to a cross, was welcome to join his kingdom. The person was more important than any category or label.

I feel convicted by this quality of Jesus every time I get involved in a cause I strongly believe in. How easy it is to join the politics of polarization, to find myself shouting across the picket lines at the "enemy" on the other side. How hard it is to remember that the kingdom of God calls me to love the woman who has just emerged from the abortion clinic (and, yes, even her doctor), the promiscuous person who is dying of AIDS, the wealthy landowner who is exploiting God's creation. If I cannot show love to such people, then I need to ask if I have understood Jesus' gospel.

A political movement by nature draws lines, makes distinctions, pronounces judgment; in contrast, Jesus' love cuts across lines, transcends distinctions, and dispenses grace. If my activism drives out such love, I betray his kingdom.

Not long ago, I attended a play based on stories from a support group comprising people with AIDS. The theater director said he decided to stage the play after hearing a local minister state that he celebrated each time he read an obituary of a young single man, believing each death to be yet another sign of God's disapproval. Increasingly, I fear, the church is viewed as an enemy of sinners.

How does one hold to high standards of moral purity while at the same time showing grace to those who fail those standards? Christian history offers few facsimiles of the pattern Jesus laid down. We give lip service to "hate the sin while loving the sinner," but how well do we practice this principle? All too often, sinners feel unloved by a church that, in turn, keeps altering its definition of sin—precisely the opposite of Jesus' pattern.

The early church began well, placing a high premium on moral purity. Baptismal candidates had to undergo long periods of instruction, and church discipline was rigorously enforced. Yet even pagan observers were attracted to the way Christians cared for each other and devoted themselves to the sick and the poor.

A major change took place with the emperor Constantine, who first legalized Christianity and made it a state-subsidized religion. At the time, his reign appeared to be the faith's greatest triumph: the emperor was now using state funds to build churches and sponsor theological conferences rather than to persecute Christians for not worshiping him. Sadly, the triumph did not come without cost. The state began appointing bishops and other church offices, and a hierarchy grew up that neatly replicated the hierarchy of the empire itself. Christian bishops began imposing morality on society at large.

I realize, as I reflect on the life of Jesus, how far we have come from the divine balance he set out for us. Listening to the sermons and reading the writings of the contemporary church in the U.S., I sometimes detect more of Constantine than of Jesus. The man from Nazareth was a sinless friend of sinners, a pattern that should convict us on both counts.

—from *Finding God in Unexpected Places*

Abounding Grace for Abounding Work

ANDREW MURRAY

It is often thought that grace and good works are at variance with each other. This is not so. What Scripture calls the works of the law, our own works, the works of righteousness which we have done, dead works—works by which we seek to merit or to be made fit for God's favour, these are indeed the very opposite of grace. But they are also the very opposite of the good works which spring from grace, and for which alone grace is bestowed. As irreconcilable as are the works of the law with the freedom of grace, so essential and indispensable are the works of faith, good works, to the true Christian life. God makes grace to abound, that good works may abound. The measure of true grace is tested and proved by the measure of good works. God's grace abounds in us that we may abound in good works. We need to have the truth deeply rooted in us: Abounding grace has *abounding work for its aim.*

And abounding work needs *abounding grace as its source and strength.* There often is abounding work without abounding grace. Just as any man may be very diligent in an earthly pursuit, or a heathen in his religious service of an idol, so men may be very diligent in doing religious work in their own strength, with but little thought of that grace which alone can do true, spiritual effective work. For all work that is to be really acceptable to God, and truly fruitful, not only for some visible result here on earth, but for eternity, the grace of God is indispensable. Paul continually speaks of his own work as owing everything to the grace of God working in him: "I laboured more abundantly than they all: yet not I, but the grace of God which was with me"(1 Cor. 15:10 KJV). "According to the gift of the grace of God given to me by the effective working of His power" (Eph. 3:7). And he as frequently calls upon Christians to exercise their gifts "according to the grace that is given us" (Rom. 12:6). "The grace given according to the measure of the gift of Christ" (Eph. 4:7). It is only by the grace of God working in us that we can do what are truly good works. It is only as we seek and receive abounding grace that we can abound in every good work.

"God is able to make all grace abound unto you, that ye may abound in all good works." With what thanksgiving every Christian ought to praise God for the abounding grace that is thus provided for him. And with what humiliation to confess that the experience of, and the surrender to, that abounding grace has been so defective. And with what confidence to believe that a life abounding in good works is indeed possible, because the abounding grace for it is so sure and so Divinely sufficient.

And then, with what simple childlike dependence to wait upon God day by day to receive the more grace which He gives to the humble.

Child of God! do take time to study and truly apprehend God's purpose with you, *that you abound in every good work!* He means it! He has provided for it! Make the measure of your consecration to Him nothing less than His purpose for you. And claim, then, nothing less than the abounding grace He is able to bestow. Make His omnipotence and His faithfulness your confidence. And live ever in the practice of continual prayer and dependence upon His power working in you. This will make you abound in every good work. According to your faith be it unto you.

Christian worker, learn here the secret of all failure and all success. Work in our own strength, with little prayer and waiting on God for His spirit, is the cause of failure. The cultivation of the spirit of absolute impotence and unceasing dependence will open the heart for the workings of the abounding grace. We shall learn to ascribe all we do to God's grace. We shall learn to measure all we have to do by God's grace. And our life will increasingly be in the joy of God's making His grace to abound in us, and our abounding in every good work.

—from *Working for God!*

Grace to Others

JERRY BRIDGES

Grace is not only to be received by us, it is, in a sense, to be extended to others. I say "in a sense" because our relationship to other people is different from God's relationship to us. He is the infinitely superior Judge and moral Governor of the universe. We are all sinners and are on an equal plane with one another. So we cannot exercise grace as God does, but we can relate to one another as those who have received grace and who wish to operate on the principles of grace.

In fact, we will not experience the peace with God and the joy of God if we are not willing to extend grace to others. This is the point of Jesus' parable of the unmerciful servant in Matthew 18:23–34. He told the story of a man who was forgiven a debt of ten thousand talents (millions of dollars), but who was unwilling to forgive a fellow servant who owed him a hundred denarii (a few dollars). The unstated truth in the parable, of course, is that our debt of sin to God is "millions of dollars," whereas the debt of others to us is, by comparison, only a few dollars.

The person living by grace sees this vast contrast between his own sins against God and the offenses of others against him. He forgives others because he himself has been so graciously forgiven. He realizes that, by receiving God's forgiveness through Christ, he has forfeited the right to be offended when others hurt him. He practices the admonition of Paul, in Ephesians 4:32: "Be kind and compassionate to one another, forgiving each other, just as in Christ God forgave you" (NIV).

—from *Transforming Grace*

Grace at Work

CHARLES SPURGEON

We must joyfully accept both repentance and remission; they cannot be separated. The covenant heritage is one and indivisible, and must not be parceled out. To divide the work of grace would be to cut the living child in halves, and those who would permit this have no interest in it.

I will ask you who are seeking the Lord, whether you would be satisfied with one of these mercies alone? Would it content you, my reader, if God would forgive you your sin and then allow you to be as worldly and wicked as before? Oh, no! The quickened spirit is more afraid of sin itself than of the penal results of it. The cry of your heart is not, "Who shall deliver me from punishment?" but, "O wretched man that I am! Who shall deliver me from the body of this death? Who shall enable me to live above temptation, and to become holy, even as God is holy?" Since the unity of repentance with remission agrees with gracious desire, and since it is necessary for the completeness of salvation, and for holiness' sake, rest you sure that it abides. . . .

When we are sure that we are forgiven, then we abhor iniquity; and I suppose that when faith grows into full assurance, so that we are certain beyond a doubt that the blood of Jesus has washed us whiter than snow, it is then that repentance reaches to its greatest height. Repentance grows as faith grows. Do not make any mistake about it; repentance is not a thing of days and weeks, a temporary penance to be over as fast as possible! No; it is the grace of a lifetime, like faith itself. God's little children repent, and so do the young men and the fathers. Repentance is the inseparable companion of faith. All the while that we walk by faith and not by sight, the tear of repentance glitters in the eye of faith. That is not true repentance which does not come of faith in Jesus, and that is not true faith in Jesus which is not tinctured with repentance. Faith and repentance, like Siamese twins, are vitally joined together. In proportion as we believe in the forgiving love of Christ, in that proportion we repent; and in proportion as we repent of sin and hate evil, we rejoice in the fullness of the absolution which Jesus is exalted to bestow. You will never value pardon unless you feel repentance; and you will never taste the deepest draught of repentance until you know that you are pardoned. It may seem a strange thing, but so it is—the bitterness of repentance and the sweetness of pardon blend in the flavor of every gracious life, and make up an incomparable happiness.

These two covenant gifts are the mutual assurance of each other. If I know that I repent, I know that I am forgiven. How am I to know that I am forgiven except I know also that I am turned from my former sinful course? To be a believer is to be a penitent. Faith and repentance are but two spokes in the same wheel, two handles of the same plough. Repentance has been well described as a heart broken *for* sin, and *from* sin; and it may equally well be spoken of as turning and returning. It is a change of mind of the most thorough and radical sort, and it is attended with sorrow for the past, and a resolve of amendment in the future.

Now, when that is the case, we may be certain that we are forgiven; for the Lord never made a heart to be broken for sin and broken from sin, without pardoning it. If, on the other hand, we are enjoying pardon, through the blood of Jesus, and are justified by faith, and have peace with God, through Jesus Christ our Lord, we know that our repentance and faith are of the right sort.

Do not regard your repentance as the cause of your remission, but as the companion of it. Do not expect to be able to repent until you see the grace of our Lord Jesus, and His readiness to blot out your sin. Keep these blessed things in their places, and view them in their relation to each other. They are the Jachin and Boaz of a saving experience; I mean that they are comparable to Solomon's two great pillars which stood in the forefront of the house of the Lord, and formed a majestic entrance to the holy place. No man comes to God aright except he passes between the pillars of repentance and remission. Upon your heart the rainbow of covenant grace has been displayed in all its beauty when the tear-drops of repentance have been shone upon by the light of full forgiveness. Repentance of sin and faith in divine pardon are the warp and woof of the fabric of real conversion.

To come back to the Scripture upon which we are meditating: both forgiveness and repentance flow from the same source, and are given by the same Saviour. The Lord Jesus in His glory bestows both upon the same persons. You are neither to find the remission nor the repentance elsewhere. Jesus has both ready, and He is prepared to bestow them now, and to bestow them most freely on all who will accept them at His hands. Let it never be forgotten that Jesus gives all that is needful for our salvation. It is highly important that all seekers after mercy should remember this. Faith is as much the gift of God as is the Saviour upon whom that faith relies. Repentance of sin is as truly the work of grace as the making of an atonement by which sin is blotted out. Salvation, from first to last, is of grace alone. You will not misunderstand me. It is not the Holy Spirit who repents. He has never done anything for which He should repent. If He could repent, it would not meet the case; we must ourselves repent of our own sin, or we are not saved from its power. It is not the Lord Jesus Christ who repents. What should He repent of? We ourselves repent with the full consent of every faculty of our mind. The will, the affections, the emotions, all work together most heartily in the blessed act of repentance for sin; and yet at the back of all that is our personal act, there is a secret holy influence which melts the heart, gives contrition, and produces a complete change. The Spirit of God enlightens us to see what sin is, and thus makes it loathsome in our eyes. The Spirit of God also turns us toward holiness, makes us heartily to appreciate, love, and desire it, and thus gives us the impetus by which we are led onward from stage to stage of sanctification. The Spirit of God works in us to will and to do according to God's good pleasure. To that good Spirit let us submit ourselves at once, that He may lead us to Jesus, who will freely give us the double benediction of repentance and remission, according to the riches of His grace.

—from *All of Grace*

The Potter and the Clay

GEORGE WHITEFIELD

Why will you not rather bring your clay to this heavenly Potter, and say from your inmost souls, "Turn us, O good Lord, and so shall we be turned?" This, you may and can do: and if you go thus far, who knows but that this very day, yea this very hour, the heavenly Potter may take you in hand, and make you vessels of honor fit for the Redeemer's use? Others that were once as far from the kingdom of God as you are, have been partakers of this blessedness. What a wretched creature was Mary Magdalene? And yet out of her Jesus Christ cast seven devils. Nay, He appeared to her first, after He rose from the dead, and she became as it were an apostle to the very apostles. What a covetous creature was Zaccheus? He was a griping cheating publican; and yet, perhaps, in one quarter of an hour's time, his heart is enlarged, and he made quite willing to give half of his goods to feed the poor. And to mention no more, what a cruel person was Paul. He was a persecutor, a blasphemer, injurious; one that breathed out threatenings against the disciples of the Lord, and made havoc of the church of Christ. And yet what a wonderful turn did he meet with, as he was journeying to Damascus? From a persecutor, he became a preacher; was afterwards made a spiritual father to thousands, and now probably sits nearest the Lord Jesus Christ in glory. And why all this? That he might be made an example to them that should hereafter believe. O then believe, repent; I beseech you, believe the gospel. Indeed, it is glad tidings, even tidings of great joy.

You, that have in some degree experienced the quickening influence (for I must not conclude without dropping a word or two to God's children) you know how to pity, and therefore, I beseech you also to pray for those, to whose circumstances this discourse is peculiarly adapted. But will you be content in praying for them? Will you not see reason to pray for yourselves also? Yes, doubtless, for yourselves also. For you, and you only know, how much there is yet lacking in your faith, and how far you are from being partakers in that degree, which you desire to be, of the whole mind that was in Christ Jesus. You know what a body of sin and death you carry about with you, and that you must necessarily expect many turns of God's providence and grace, before you will be wholly delivered from it. But thanks be to God, we are in safe hands. He that has been the author, will also be the finisher of our faith. Yet a little while, and we like Him shall say "It is finished"; we shall bow down our heads and give up the ghost. Till then, (for to Thee, O Lord, will we now direct our prayer) help us, O Almighty Father, in patience to possess our souls. Behold, we are the clay, and Thou art the Potter. Let not the thing formed say to Him that formed it, whatever the dispensations of Thy future Will concerning us may be, Why dost Thou deal with us thus? Behold, we put ourselves as blanks in Thine hands, deal with us as seemeth good in Thy sight, only let every cross, every affliction, every temptation, be overruled to the stamping Thy blessed image in more lively characters on our hearts; that so passing from glory to glory, by the powerful operations of Thy blessed

Spirit, we may be made thereby more and more meet for, and at last be translated to a full, perfect, endless, and uninterrupted enjoyment of glory hereafter, with Thee O Father, Thee O Son, and Thee O blessed Spirit; to whom, three persons but one God, be ascribed, as is most due, all honor, power, might, majesty and dominion, now and to all eternity. Amen and Amen.

—from *Selected Sermons of George Whitefield*

Make Me an Instrument

FRANCIS OF ASSISI

Lord, make me an instrument of your peace.

Where there is injury, let me bring pardon;

where there is hatred, love,

where there is doubt, faith,

where there is despair, hope,

where there is darkness, light,

where there is sadness, joy.

O Divine Master, grant that I may not seek so much

to be consoled as to console,

to be understood as to understand,

to be loved as to love;

for it is in giving that we receive,

it is in pardoning that we are pardoned,

and it is in dying that we are born to eternal life.

Notes

HOW SWEET THE SOUND

1. Donald W. McCullough, *Waking from the American Dream* (Downers Grove, Ill.: InterVarsity Press, 1988), p. 116.
2. C. F. D. Moule, *An Idiom Book of New Testament Greek* (New York: Cambridge University Press, 1959), p. 44.

JESUS: THE PERSON OF GRACE

1. Nicholson and Lee, eds. *The Oxford Book of English Mystical Verse* (Oxford: The Clarendon Press, 1971).

BY GRACE ALONE

1. Edward Mote, "The Solid Rock."

Acknowledgments

Grateful acknowledgment is made to the following publishers and copyright holders for permission to reprint copyrighted material:

James Montgomery Boice, for material on pages 15–16, 154–156. Taken from *The Glory of God's Grace* © 1993 by James Montgomery Boice. Published by Kregel Publications, Grand Rapids, MI. Used by permission of the publisher. All rights reserved.

Dietrich Bonhoeffer. Reprinted with the permission of Scribner, an imprint of Simon & Schuster Adult Publishing Group, from THE COST OF DISCIPLESHIP by Dietrich Bonhoeffer. Copyright © 1959 by SCM Press Ltd.

Jerry Bridges. Reprinted from *Transforming Grace*, © 1991 by Jerry Bridges. Used by permission of NavPress, Colorado Springs, CO. All rights reserved.

Michael Card. Excerpted from *A Violent Grace* © 2000 by Michael Card. Used by permission of Multnomah Publishers, Inc.

Amy Carmichael. From *Edges of His Ways* by Amy Carmichael, copyright © 1955 Dohnavur Fellowship. Published by CLC Publications, Fort Washington, PA. Used by permission.

—From *Toward Jerusalem* by Amy Carmichael, copyright © 1936 Dohnavur Fellowship. Published by CLC Publications, Fort Washington, PA. Used by permission.

C. S. Lewis. THE LAST BATTLE, by C. S. Lewis copyright © C. S. Lewis Pte. Ltd. 1956. Extract reprinted by permission.

Max Lucado. Reprinted by permission. *A Gentle Thunder*, Max Lucado, copyright date 2002, W Publishing, Nashville, Tennessee. All rights reserved.

—Reprinted by permission. *The Great House of God*, Max Lucado, copyright date 2001, Word Publishing, Nashville, Tennessee. All rights reserved.

—Reprinted by permission. *He Still Moves Stones*, Max Lucado, copyright date 1999, Word Publishing, Nashville, Tennessee. All rights reserved.

—Reprinted by permission. *In the Grip of Grace,* Max Lucado, copyright date 1996, Word Publishing, Nashville, Tennessee. All rights reserved.

Brennan Manning. Excerpted from *The Ragamuffin Gospel* © 1990, 2000 by Brennan Manning. Used by permission of Multnomah Publishers, Inc.

—Material on pages 199–201 from the following source: Pages 55–8, 63–4 from THE WISDOM OF TENDERNESS by BRENNAN MANNING. Copyright © 2002 by Brennan Manning. Reprinted by permission of HarperCollins Publishers Inc.

Brian D. McLaren, for material on page 23. Taken from FINDING FAITH by BRIAN D. MCLAREN. Copyright © 1999 by Brian D. McLaren. Used by permission of the Zondervan Corporation.

Kathleen Norris. "Grace," from AMAZING GRACE by Kathleen Norris, copyright © 1998 by Kathleen Norris. Used by permission of Riverhead Books, an imprint of Penguin Group (USA) Inc.